Professional Doctorates: Integrating Professional and Academic Knowledge

SRHE and Open University Press Imprint
General Editor: Heather Eggins

Current titles include:

Catherine Bargh *et al.*: *University Leadership*
Ronald Barnett: *Beyond all Reason*
Ronald Barnett: *The Limits of Competence*
Ronald Barnett: *Higher Education*
Ronald Barnett: *Realizing the University in an Age of Supercomplexity*
Tony Becher and Paul R. Trowler: *Academic Tribes and Territories (2nd edn)*
Neville Bennett *et al.*: *Skills Development in Higher Education and Employment*
John Biggs: *Teaching for Quality Learning at University (2nd edn)*
Richard Blackwell & Paul Blackmore (eds): *Towards Strategic Staff Development in Higher Education*
David Boud *et al.* (eds): *Using Experience for Learning*
David Boud and Nicky Solomon (eds): *Work-based Learning*
Tom Bourner *et al.* (eds): *New Directions in Professional Higher Education*
John Brennan *et al.* (eds): *What Kind of University?*
Anne Brockbank and Ian McGill: *Facilitating Reflective Learning in Higher Education*
Stephen D. Brookfield and Stephen Preskill: *Discussion as a Way of Teaching*
Ann Brooks and Alison Mackinnon (eds): *Gender and the Restructured University*
Sally Brown and Angela Glasner (eds): *Assessment Matters in Higher Education*
James Cornford & Neil Pollock: *Putting the University Online*
John Cowan: *On Becoming an Innovative University Teacher*
Sarah Delamont, Paul Atkinson and Odette Parry: *Supervising the PhD*
Sarah Delamont & Paul Atkinson: *Research Cultures and Careers*
Gerard Delanty: *Challenging Knowledge*
Chris Duke: *Managing the Learning University*
Heather Eggins (ed.): *Globalization and Reform in Higher Education*
Heather Eggins & Ranald Macdonald (eds): *The Scholarship of Academic Development*
Gillian Evans: *Academics and the Real World*
Andrew Hannan and Harold Silver: *Innovating in Higher Education*
Lee Harvey and Associates: *The Student Satisfaction Manual*
David Istance, Hans Schuetze and Tom Schuller (eds): *International Perspectives on Lifelong Learning*
Norman Jackson and Helen Lund (eds): *Benchmarking for Higher Education*
Merle Jacob and Tomas Hellström (eds): *The Future of Knowledge Production in the Academy*
Peter Knight: *Being a Teacher in Higher Education*
Peter Knight and Paul Trowler: *Departmental Leadership in Higher Education*
Peter Knight and Mantz Yorke: Assessment, Learning and Employability
Mary Lea and Barry Stierer (eds): *Student Writing in Higher Education*
Ian McNay (ed.): *Higher Education and its Communities*
Elaine Martin: *Changing Academic Work*
Louise Morley: *Quality and Power in Higher Education*
Moira Peelo and Terry Wareham (eds): *Failing Students in Higher Education*
Craig Prichard: *Making Managers in Universities and Colleges*
Michael Prosser and Keith Trigwell: *Understanding Learning and Teaching*
John Richardson: *Researching Student Learning*
Stephen Rowland: *The Enquiring University Teacher*
Maggi Savin-Baden: *Problem-based Learning in Higher Education*
Maggi Savin-Baden: *Facilitating Problem-based Learning*
David Scott, Andrew Brown, Ingrid Lunt & Lucy Thorne: Professional Doctorates: Integrating Professional and Academic Knowledge
Peter Scott (ed.): *The Globalization of Higher Education*
Peter Scott: *The Meanings of Mass Higher Education*
Michael L Shattock: *Managing Successful Universities*

Maria Slowey and David Watson: *Higher Education and the Lifecourse*
Anthony Smith and Frank Webster (eds): *The Postmodern University?*
Colin Symes and John McIntyre (eds): *Working Knowledge*
Peter G. Taylor: *Making Sense of Academic Life*
Richard Taylor, Jean Barr and Tom Steele: *For a Radical Higher Education*
Malcolm Tight: *Researching Higher Education*
Penny Tinkler and Carolyn Jackson: *The Doctoral Examination Process*
Susan Toohey: *Designing Courses for Higher Education*
Paul R. Trowler (ed.): *Higher Education Policy and Institutional Change*
Melanie Walker (ed.): *Reconstructing Professionalism in University Teaching*
David Warner and David Palfreyman (eds): *Higher Education Management of UK Higher Education*
Gareth Williams (ed.): *The Enterprising University*
Diana Woodward and Karen Ross: *Managing Equal Opportunities in Higher Education*

Professional Doctorates: Integrating Professional and Academic Knowledge

David Scott, Andrew Brown, Ingrid Lunt and Lucy Thorne

Society for Research into Higher Education
& Open University Press

Open University Press
McGraw-Hill Education
McGraw-Hill House
Shoppenhangers Road
Maidenhead
Berkshire
England
SL6 2QL

email: enquiries@openup.co.uk
world wide web: www.openup.co.uk

and Two Penn Plaza, New York, NY 10121-2289, USA

First published 2004

Copyright © The Authors, 2004

A catalogue record of this book is available from the British Library

ISBN 0 335 21332 4 (pb)   0 335 21333 2 (hb)

Library of Congress Cataloging-in-Publication Data
CIP data applied for

Typeset by RefineCatch Limited, Bungay, Suffolk
Printed in the UK by Bell & Bain Ltd, Glasgow

Contents

Acknowledgements

This book has its origins in an Economic and Social Research Council project (no. R000223643) entitled 'Professional Doctorates and Professional Development in Education'. The aim of the research was to provide new insights into the nature of professional doctorates and their relationships with the workplace. It attempted to answer four questions: (1) How does the professional doctorate in education, engineering and business administration influence participants' professional lives and act to develop professional knowledge and improve practice? (2) What is the impact of the development of professional knowledge on the employment culture of the students? (3) How do universities organize doctoral level programmes that facilitate professional learning and development, and what pedagogical and organizational strategies are used? *and* (4) What is the most appropriate relationship between professional and academic knowledge, and how can universities develop practice which best reflects this? Our thinking, reflected, we hope, in this book, has moved beyond these four questions. No new data were collected for the book. It is in this context that we acknowledge the contribution of tutors, students and graduates in the 12 universities that provided us with our data-set. We have chosen to anonymize both the universities and the students, since many of the issues that we discuss may have consequences for the participants arising from this publication. Because we have chosen not to name institutions and students, this should not detract from our gratitude to those places and people for their help with the research. Finally, we presented some of our initial findings at a conference on professional doctorates at the University of Queensland in December 2002. This was subsequently published in the Conference Proceedings (Scott *et al.* 2003), and forms the basis of Chapter 4.

1

Introduction

At first glance this is a book about practising professionals engaging in the rewarding, but difficult and often frustrating, business of completing a higher professional degree at a university. It is though more than this as its central theme is the dissonance between two cultures of learning, and the way students undertaking higher professional degrees have to confront the seeming irreducibility of the one to the other. It is therefore about peripherality, assimilation, learning and achievement. It is also about the different ways the *student-practitioner* is constructed within workplace and academic cultures, and how in an attempt to mediate between the two, they make choices that allow them to make sense of their lives.

Professional doctorates exist in the twilight zone between the university and the workplace. In this book we examine the changing role of the university, and in particular we focus on courses offered by the university for the development of professional learning. An implicit assumption made by members of a university is that when they offer professional development courses, the knowledge, skills and dispositions that make up those courses will lead to improvements to the various practices to which they make reference. However, we do not suggest that higher education learning transfers unproblematically to the workplace, despite the frequent assertions in course brochures and the like that this is what is intended. Professional learning, caught in the cusp between the two worlds, is a complex matter. Besides, workplace outcomes from professional development courses are difficult to identify, and especially so from courses of the type that we are dealing with here, and we might even be tempted to suggest that in some cases the schooled practitioner is less well equipped to go on in the workplace. What follows is an attempt to come to terms with an important development in the business of universities and in particular their desire to build bridges between themselves and the world of work.

The growth of professional doctorates in the UK

The subject matter of the book is the professional doctorate, and we offer here a brief history of its development in UK universities. In the past ten years there have been major changes in the nature of the university, the kind and numbers of participants in higher education, and the role of the university for higher professional development (cf. Barnett 1999). The end of the binary divide, the rapid increase in student numbers and postgraduate programmes, the moves to 'lifelong learning' (Watson 2000) and the professions' own focus on continuing professional development (Becher 1999b) have all changed the profile of the university. Higher education is thus being brought into closer co-operation with a wide range of other work places (Winter *et al.* 2000). The Winfield Enquiry (1987), the Harris Report (1996), the Dearing Report (1977) and a recent publication of the QAA (1999) highlight the growing political interest in postgraduate and doctoral education and exemplify concerns expressed over quality and standards of awards. It is in this context that the rapid growth in numbers of professional and practice-based doctorates is giving rise to significant questions about the nature and purposes of doctoral education and the relationship between these more recent doctorates and the traditional PhD (Bourner *et al.* 2000a).

There has also been a change for the professions themselves; many have increased their qualification requirements, and for some (for example clinical psychologists) this has meant a move towards doctoral programmes for initial qualification (Holland and Brown 2000). Within the professions, requirements for greater accountability and a rapidly changing environment have led to an interest in 'reflective practice' (Schon 1987), 'critical reflection' and experiential learning within continuing professional development (Boud and Walker 1990; Brookfield 1995). The doctorate degree in the UK is therefore no longer only an academic qualification, but also a professional, and in some cases a vocational qualification. At the same time there have been strong moves to make the PhD itself more vocational (for example Collinson 1998).

These factors have contributed to a widespread development of professional doctorates in the UK (Bourner *et al.* 2000a), following developments in the USA where they have existed for many years (Noble 1994), and Australia (Maxwell and Shanahan 2000). This forms part of a general expansion of higher degrees for a wider range of student (Jarvis 2000). Although there are a small number of vocational (initial training) doctorates in the UK (for example, clinical psychologists), professional and practice-based doctorates were introduced during the 1990s mainly to provide a higher qualification for already experienced practitioners in a range of fields, for example, the EngD for qualified engineers, the DBA for senior managers, and the EdD for senior education professionals (Becher 1999a).

The complex and contested relationship between what constitutes academic and professional knowledge, particularly within the context of a professional doctorate in education (Scott and Lunt 2000) highlights some of the problems with equating academic and practitioner knowledge, and points to the particular challenges to universities developing teaching and learning for professional doctorates. A number of different models have been developed for the provision of such programmes, and universities have developed a range of flexible learning approaches, which emphasize active roles for students and interactive and collegial processes throughout the teaching and learning programmes. Indeed, the tension between the professional objectives of some EdD programmes and academic evaluation criteria has given rise to a range of innovative practices that challenge orthodox conceptions of doctoral study (see, for instance, Baumgart and Linfoot 1998).

The emergence of professional doctorates in the UK reflects a number of pressures within the professions and in universities. There is a perceived need for professionals to engage in higher professional development, to reflect critically on their practice, to develop transferable skills and competencies, and to gain higher qualifications. On the other hand, there is a pressure for universities to diversify, and to offer more professionally relevant programmes. In response to this, professional doctorates have developed rapidly over the past decade. The EdD was introduced in the UK to meet the demand from a growing market; the first programme was offered in 1992. It is now one of the more established professional doctorates in the country; and is offered by about 36 universities. The EngD was also first offered in 1992, as a result of an initiative by the Engineering and Physical Sciences Research Council. This body funded studentships initially in three universities, followed by two more, and, following a review of the programme, a further five in 1997. Recently, professional doctorates have been offered in Business Administration (DBA), Pharmacy (DPharm), Educational Psychology (DEdPsy), and a growing number of professional areas. While the university programmes vary considerably in their target students, structure, approaches to curriculum, pedagogy, assessment, and their professional ethos, they also have a number of elements in common. Developing an understanding of this very different form of higher professional development, and the kind of knowledge and research generated through these programmes is necessary to a consideration of the needs of pre-service and mid-career professionals (Burgess 1997).

In the UK, with moves for the PhD to become more vocational and for the first year to be structured through taught courses, it is possible to understand this as what might be termed the professionalization of the doctorate. However, this raises a number of concerns, such as how doctoral degrees are able to contribute to higher professional development, and how a common understanding of issues such as parity, standards, pedagogy and professional knowledge can be achieved by a range of institutions in the UK and indeed worldwide. Thorne (1999) has demonstrated that there is a significant divergence in the views of doctorates and doctoral graduates held by employers, supervisors and the doctoral candidates themselves. She argues further (Thorne 2001), that the traditional concept of customization associated with the PhD is and must be treated problematically for professional doctorates, in order that they are valued by relevant organizations and professional bodies, as well as academia. The strong claims to support professional development, made particularly by the EdD, highlight the specific need to explore the perceptions of employers and professional colleagues, in any attempt to develop a common understanding of what constitutes learning of this kind.

The study

We have chosen to focus on three of these professional doctorates: the Doctorate in Business Administration, the Education Doctorate and the Engineering Doctorate. The rationale for this selection is that these three professional doctorate programmes were some of the first to be offered in the UK, and currently have more students and graduates than with the more recent programmes.

Our approach has been to collect fine-grained and multi-faceted data on each of 12 programmes. Guided by earlier surveys of professional doctorates in Great Britain (for example, Scott and Lunt 2000; Bourner, Bowden and Laing 2001a) and our own knowledge of the field of professional doctorates, we selected four examples of each type of programme in an attempt to encompass within the sample the range of current practice in each area. The resulting multi-site examination of different programme types and analysis of the pedagogical and workplace contexts of the professional learners enabled us to build 12 detailed case studies of professional doctorate programmes. These 12 case studies provide the basis for the observations and arguments presented in this book, and we use material collected to illustrate, support and challenge the points made. Our principle motivation in collecting and analysing this case study material has been to generate a better understanding of the phenomenon of the professional doctorate and of variation within and between programmes.

The principal methods of data collection were individual and group semi-structured interviews with the key stakeholders – the professional doctorate participants (current students and graduates); the participants' professional community (employers and professional colleagues); and the professional doctorate tutors (programme directors, module leaders and student supervisors). Case study visits were made to 12 universities, and these covered four exemplars of each of the three programme types (DBA, EdD and EngD). Interviews were carried out with key informants; these were followed up by telephone interviews with programme participants and graduates. The interviews were recorded and transcribed. Field notes provided additional contextual detail. We also collected programme materials, which included promotional literature and pedagogic resources used by tutors. These and the interview transcriptions formed the main data-sets for the analysis. In addressing the question of the organizational features of the programmes and the pedagogic strategies employed, published and unpublished information about the programmes (including prospectuses and course material) was collected, alongside interviews with tutors working on the programmes and with students. The main focus was on understanding the three types of programmes and their relationships with professional practice from the various individual and group perspectives.

Previous research and writing on professional doctorates has either focused on the specific characteristics of these programmes in comparison to more conventional PhDs (for example Maxwell and Shanahan 1997, 2000; Bourner *et al.* 2000a), or has taken the growth of professional doctorates as an indicator of a shift in modes of the production of knowledge (for example Lee *et al.* 2000). The empirical components of such studies have taken the form of either a survey (Maxwell and Shanahan 1997, for example, investigated the balance between taught and research components of EdD programmes in Australia), or the selection of particular cases to support an argument or exemplify a position (Lee *et al.* 2000 selected two Doctor of Business administration programmes in order to explore differences in the nature of knowledge produced within professional doctorate and conventional PhD programmes).

The study of pedagogical, organizational and knowledge-development strategies presented here differs from previous work in two key respects. First, an attempt was made, by looking in detail at a range of professional doctorates (in Engineering, Business Administration and Education), to identify similarities and differences within and between different forms of professional doctorate. Second, for each of the cases studied, a variety of forms of data representing different perspectives and positions was collected (including documents relating to the programmes and interviews with tutors, participants, graduates and their workplace colleagues). Whilst previous studies have tended to homogenize professional doctorates, this study is able to present both the distinctive character of the professional doctorate and to explore differences within and between particular domains of practice in relation to both the institutions, forms of partnership and academic disciplines involved, and the characteristics, motivations and workplace circumstances of the participants.

Topics and themes

The first part of this book focuses on contexts and relationships. Drawing on the extensive literature on Higher Education, we examine the origin of the professional doctorate, the role of the university in the modern era and its complex relations with clientele professional bodies. In particular, we explore the development of higher academic and professional degrees, the university's role in the construction of knowledge, and the positioning of the university in the reconstruction of professional knowledge within workplaces. Mindful of the variety of workplace cultures addressed in this book (engineering, business and education), we describe and problematize the way they work.

Part 2 examines the important issue of knowledge, its divisions and reconciliations. Within it we develop a typology of knowledge modes as they relate to study on a professional doctorate. We also identify various hybrid forms that have evolved out of the tension between academic and professional knowledge. In Chapter 5 we examine the idea of reflection, central to professional doctorate study. Reflection-in-action may be seen as a set of corrective competencies. This chapter explores alternative understandings of the process and critiques competency and effectiveness discourses. It shows through examination of this process in action that it is embodied and situated, and involves reconstructions of knowledge and self.

Part 3 examines issues relating to teaching and learning. In Chapter 6 we explore the marketing of the three types of professional doctorates studied, and consider the selection and assessment of participants in order to better understand variations in the sanctioned identities of participants within and between programmes. In Chapter 7 we look at the structure and curriculum of the three types of programmes and analyse the forms of pedagogy employed and the pedagogic relations established within each programme. Questions are raised here about the tendency to treat professional doctorates as a unity and suggestions are made about how we might reach a better understanding of variation within and between programmes.

Part 4 is concerned with identity, and in particular, personal and professional development. Chapter 8 examines the important issue of motivation and why students undertake professional study of this type. Within these programmes, individual students construct personal work profiles and careers. Chapter 9 examines their trajectories, and focuses in particular on the period of doctoral study and its aftermath. It also examines the issue of transferability of skills acquired during study on the doctorate, and how these relate to the construction of professional and personal identities. Finally, issues to do with professionalism, credentialism and status hierarchies are explored in Chapter 10. The three doctoral programmes central to this book are different because of their different histories and different views of knowledge, and consequently understandings of the relationship between academic and practitioner knowledge.

The last chapter draws together the various threads of the book, and provides an overall view of learning on professional doctorate courses. It also attempts an evaluation of this type of learning and how it impacts on universities and workplaces. Our first theme is the changing role of the university with regards to doctorate study.

Part 1

Histories and Contexts

2

The Changing Role of the University

Introduction

Scott (2000) identifies five attributes of the late-modern world. The first is acceleration, and he means by this both an increasing volume of intellectual, aesthetic and technological goods being placed in society, and the turnover of these goods so that they have a shorter and shorter lifespan. The second attribute he identifies is simultaneity, or as Giddens (1991) describes it, the radical compression of time–space. Fuelled by the Internet and other techno-logical compressors, this has led to forms of globalization that are having profound effects on relations between people. The third attribute is increas-ing risk and this is unavoidable given the dissolution of collective identities and loci of custom. The fourth attribute identified by Scott is non-linearity, complexity and chaos, and he means by these both that knowledge is now revisable and that it is ceaselessly revised through interaction with endlessly changing environments. His last attribute is reflexivity. Again, he suggests that this takes several forms: boundaries between producers and users of knowledge are weakened; knowledge foundations are discredited and shown to be the expressions of particular economic and valued interests; it becomes more difficult to identify progress in society; and finally, as he puts it, 'we construct our own reflexive biographies' (Scott 2000: 20). All of these have implications for the role of the university in the late-modern world, and its attempts to break free from the rigid boundaries that it imposed on itself with regards to knowledge construction and development. Professional doc-torates are one manifestation of this desire, though perhaps the driver for their development has been the need to compete in the marketplace, and to extend the disciplinary arm of the university into the world of the workplace.

To these we can add five more. The first is the way power strategies are becoming better understood and better able to be used. Indeed, those power strategies are embedded in the production of certain types of disciplinary knowledge (Green and Lee 1999). Usher *et al.* (1997: 73) suggest, for example, that with regards to the discipline of psychology, it has become as it matures 'a technology of human behaviour, a body of knowledge that is also "technically" exploitable and can be used both to regulate and change individuals and relationships'. Though it would purport to offer value-neutral descriptions of human behaviour (Foucault 1977), in effect, the discipline works to regulate and control through processes of normalization and individualization. Here, we are making the point that disciplinary knowledge embedded in universities both provides solace for its members and has powerful effects. Marshall (1990: 22) suggests that the two most obvious meanings of the word 'discipline', seemingly separate in fact are closely intertwined: 'a body of knowledge is a system of social control to the extent that discipline (knowledge) makes discipline (social control) possible and vice versa'. Race is an example of this in the sense that it has no ontological basis (Carter 2000), and yet racial classification produces social objects and has social effects. Its classificatory regime serves to control and position individuals within a discourse of ethnicity.

The second additional attribute is the reallocation of power bases within society from powerful elites including expert bodies in universities to other sources of authority. This is more than just the weakening of boundaries between forms of knowledge and between different types of knowledge producers and users, it also involves a marginalization of traditional sources of knowledge and influence, and a reallocation of that power and influence to other bodies that have a different conception of what knowledge is and what its purposes are. This has involved processes of translation (Kendall 2002) so that a practice is rewritten in the image of another. An example is the incorporation of a notion of training into PhD study from what was previously considered to be an educational process. This translation is in part achieved through a process of simplification (cf. Latour 1987), and Kendall describes it in the following way:

> A hard-to-define term is replaced by a simple one; the uncertainties and messiness of education are transformed into the simple three-year training, with precisely ordered and named parts (Review, Methodology, Experiments, Analysis). The image for which doctoral education is rewritten must also be simplified: hence we see unsophisticated and simplistic models of 'society' ('knowledge society'), 'progress' ('good training will lead to an economically healthy nation'), 'citizen' ('knowledge workers') and 'capital' ('tangible assets') used as the point of reference.
>
> (2002: 138)

This discursive sleight-of-hand is also reinforced by the imposition of sanctions which act to reconfigure the way these matters are understood and position individuals as a part of the discourse.

The third additional attribute is that control is exercised at a distance by governing elites. This distancing mechanism works by giving individual institutions the responsibility to make decisions about their future but then at the same time setting in place arrangements by which those practices are monitored and evaluated. If institutions do not meet the requirements of these quasi-governmental bodies, then they are subject to financial and other sanctions. This is different from direct control over their activities or from creating a discursive regime that makes it difficult to step outside those ways of thinking sanctioned from above.

The fourth additional attribute is compartmentalization. The person compartmentalizes aspects of their life, so that an academic may offer in their published writings radical and transformative accounts of educational processes, and yet adopt within their working lives as senior managers in institutions ways of working and arrangements for subordinates which both reinforce the status quo and contradict their beliefs. These strategies are an addendum to the self-reflexive strategies adopted by them as a consequence of being cast adrift from universal and/or local forms of identity. Finally, there is a process of commodification in relation to knowledge. Here, knowledge of processes, institutions and selves is reconfigured so that it becomes a sellable property. Its value is its usefulness as a good to be exchanged in the marketplace.

These ten attributes serve to distinguish modern societies from late-modern societies, and have had a profound effect on the way universities go about their business. Acceleration and turnover, time–space compression, increasing risk, non-linearity, reflexivity, normalization and individualization, the marginalization of traditional forms of knowledge and the reallocation of power bases, evaluation at a distance, compartmentalization and commodification are significant processes in the transformation of the university. In turn, the university itself is increasingly being influenced by policy-driven interventions of the state, new forms of communication, its marginalization from the centre of the knowledge industry, 'non-jurisdictionally bounded global discourses' (Yeatman 1990) and by crises in disciplinarity and professionalism (Brennan 1998). Moreover, the introduction of professional doctorates in the UK context signals a move by both the university and the professions to reconfigure what is considered appropriate research and practice knowledge. Yeatman (1996) identifies three kinds of knowledge: knowledge of how to use theoretical analysis and scientifically orientated empirical research; knowledge of how to reflect on the requirements of the practice and practice setting in question; and knowledge of how to work with 'service users' to deliver and improve the service concerned. These reflect a tension between 'theory-orientated' and 'practice-based' knowledges (Eraut 1994; Usher *et al.* 1997), and have implications for pedagogy at doctoral level, assessment of products, legitimation, and more generally the relationship between higher education and the continuing development of serving professionals (Lee 1999).

Academic work

Lee (1999: 8) further suggests that what works in the workplace cannot be validated by the university in terms of the logics of production currently practised in the university: 'the researcher is positioned methodologically and otherwise as a feature of the discipline itself. Knowledge produced in the context of application clearly calls for principles and processes of evaluation that go far beyond the knowledge systems of the disciplinary arm of the university.' What are the characteristics of these knowledge systems? The product is inscribed, usually at length, and this can be contrasted with workplace products that are short, focussed, mainly oral and impermanent. The university product is canonical and the student is expected to make reference to past work and reconceptualizations of past work within the discipline. The canon changes over time but still retains its aura of permanency and authority. Products are long and produced over a long timescale, and we can perhaps note here recent policy moves to compress the doctoral timescale and the way this reflects Scott's first attribute – acceleration and turnover. Work within the disciplinary arm of the university is therefore cumulative so that knowledge develops in the footsteps of previous theories and ideas. Radical breaks though possible are rarely encouraged, and at PhD level, positively dangerous for the novitiate as their work is judged by a paradigm laboriously built up by the work of others in the discipline.

The writer/researcher/academic writes him- or herself out of the picture so that this form of knowledge is characterized by a detachment from the subject matter. The person's beliefs, orientations and interests are considered to be marginal to the production of this form of knowledge. This can be compared with forms of de-distancing that are prevalent in professional doctorates. Abstraction involves a distancing from the object of study. Professional knowledge and the practicum cannot afford this distancing, so we have a de-distancing process. However, we will see that in the practice of professional doctorate study, the disciplinary arm of the university works to reassert its authority as a knowledge producer.

With this detachment goes a form of enclosure, so that the university is separated off from the rest of society, not least in terms of how its products are judged. These judgements are internal to the discipline itself through peer review, and do not embrace judgements made by the professions, business, policy makers and the like. Within this enclosed circle, there is a clear rejection of the idea that knowledge can be judged by whether it works in practice settings because this is seen as an irrelevance to the closed world of academia. Specialized vocabularies and logical forms are developed which act to exclude those who have not been initiated into the discipline. The knowledge that is developed becomes abstract, esoteric and specialized. At the same time, pedagogical processes are developed which best fit the desire to initiate new recruits to the discipline.

These can be compared with more recent developments in the university which has begun to embrace more open forms of discourse, and move from closed transmissive canonical forms of pedagogy to more open forms in which student choice, and therefore an acknowledgement of prior experiential knowledge, is allowed. These may take the form of modularity, pacing, choice of writing topic, choice of research method and the like. However, the university exercising control at a distance, still retains this, even if invisibly, through continuous and terminal forms of assessment.

Within this scenario, a number of ideas have been developed that draw the university away from its enclosed space. McNair (1997) identifies four of these. The first is the knowledge-based economy. Reich (1993) has coined the term 'symbolic analysts' to refer to a group of people who work at this form of higher order problem solving. He characterizes them in the following way:

> Symbolic analysts solve, identify and broker problems by manipulating symbols. They simplify reality into abstract images that can be rearranged, juggled, experimented with, communicated to other specialists, and then, eventually transformed back into reality. The manipulations are done with analytical tools . . . Some reveal how to more efficiently deploy resources, save time and energy. Other manipulations yield new inventions – technological marvels, innovative legal arguments, new advertising ploys. . . . Still other manipulations – of sounds, words, and pictures – serve to entertain their recipients, or cause them to reflect more deeply.
>
> (Reich 1993: 178)

This symbolic work has some affinities with traditional university agendas; however, what is being suggested is that the type of goods that fuel modern economies has in part changed from material to symbolic.

The second idea referred to by McNair is the learning organization, whereby, instead of learning being understood as external to the workplace and then imported into it, members of that organization engage in continuous and collaborative learning processes. One version of the learning organization is exemplified by Senge's (1990) model, in which he suggests that a learning organization is characterized by personal mastery, shared vision, mental models, team learning and systems thinking. Organizations therefore are coming to resemble traditional academic departments in universities in that symbolic work becomes the norm.

The third idea of McNair is globalization, and this, as we suggested, has homogenizing as well as democratic characteristics. This last is underpinned by a HyperTextual model of representation in which the introduction of new media, in particular the World Wide Web, is acting to reconfigure discursive arrangements and the place of the reader within them. Conventional models of textual production and consumption have privileged the writer over the reader. The World Wide Web has given us the possibility of, though it is as yet hardly a revolution, a more democratic relationship to the power of textual production, which works on us and not through us. Landow (1992: 70–1) coins the phrase 'this HyperTextual dissolution of centrality', and what he means by this is that new media allow the possibility of conversation rather than instruction so that no one ideology or agenda dominates any other: '. . . the figure of the HyperText author approaches, even if it does not entirely merge with, that of the reader; the functions of reader and writer become more deeply intertwined with each other than ever before'.

The fourth idea of McNair is lifelong learning, and though different people have understood this in different ways, it has had a powerful influence on contemporary policy debates. It is characterized by an emphasis on the development of experiential knowledge; the dissolution of boundaries between formal and informal schooling; the designation of the life course as a continuous and never-ending opportunity for learning; and the development of the continually changing self in response to ever changing environments. The knowledge-based economy, the learning organization, globalized democratic possibilities, and lifelong learning, though contested concepts, are beginning to change the historic mission of the university, and have influenced the development of higher professional degrees. Professional doctorates are one manifestation of this; and we need to briefly understand their genesis as they developed out of, and in parallel with, the PhD.

A brief history of the PhD

Cowan (1997: 184) coins the term 'the bureaucratisation of originality' to describe the history of the PhD from which professional doctorates have emerged, and we cannot understand the latter without reference to the former, and without reference to the changing mission and purpose of the university. The eighteenth-century concern was the preparation of an administrative elite and in particular the development of the professions. In opposition to this in Germany, the Humboldt reforms envisaged a new type of university knowledge, founded on enlightenment principles and reflecting a desire by the university to engage in a search for a form of universal truth that set it apart from society and placed itself in a position of authority with regards to the production of knowledge. Henceforth, other forms of knowledge were considered to be inferior and based on folkloric foundations.

The Humboldt reforms had the effect of placing the professor at the centre of university affairs, downgrading the power and influence of the old professional faculties of theology, law and medicine, and paradoxically elevating the philosophical faculty. In Berlin University where the Humboldt reforms had the most influence the only degree offered was the doctorate, though most students never completed it but settled for the qualifying examination for the civil service or teaching in a gymnasium (Cowan 1997). These reforms in turn led to other changes to the university's curriculum, not least the fracturing of the university into specialist groups or disciplines. The pattern in Germany had been set with a notion of the research-orientated, individually responsible, specialized search for universal forms of knowledge as the paradigm for activity within the university.

Though these reforms did not translate unproblematically into other universities round the world, they certainly influenced them, and the German ideal became a model for universities in the USA and the UK. As Cowan puts it in relation to the importation of these ideas to the USA:

> the mixture of processes – the consolidation and standardisation of the esoteric knowledge of the legal and medical professions, the redefinition of the higher education system, the specification of one of the basic units of American academic life, the department, and the importation of the doctorate with its possibilities for the certification of a profession of learning – are all visible in this period from the 1860s to 1900.
>
> (1997: 189)

This was one of the most significant developments in the evolution of the university as it signalled a system of qualification and thus control over its own kind: its teachers, students and researchers.

Impressed by the efforts of the university reforms in Germany and the USA, Oxford established a PhD in 1917, though they called it a DLitt. Other universities swiftly followed this example. The idea of a profession of learning had taken hold on universities round the world and became a significant marker for how they would be seen by insiders and outsiders alike. The doctorate in the USA gradually evolved so that it became the forerunner for the professional doctorate in Australia and the UK. It became both highly structured and as we will see bureaucratized. In effect, it embraced four elements: a taught component; a sequenced series of points of progression through a programme; a course committee to oversee the work of the student, and thus we should note the absence of single professorial control; and a shorter dissertation embracing a measure of transparency of method (Cowan 1997).

In turn in the UK and elsewhere, this led to national standards and formal procedures for doctoral completion, and processes of national control over production. Sanctions were imposed on universities if they failed to achieve a percentage rate of completions within a set timescale. For example, the Quality Assurance Agency for Higher Education in the UK produced a code of practice for the assurance of academic quality and standards for postgraduate research programmes (QAA 1999). The document develops a list of precepts to which higher education institutions are expected to conform, even if they do not follow the guidance outlined in the same paper. The precepts refer to general principles, the research environment, promotional information, the selection and admission of students, enrolment and registration of research students, student information and induction, the approval of research projects, skills training, supervision, assessment, feedback, complaints and appeals, and institutional evaluation. The result is, as Cowan (1997: 196) makes clear, 'an increasing bureaucratisation within doctoral programmes; of pedagogic sequence; of pedagogic relations, through memoranda; and of knowledge, into training modules'.

In line with this increasing bureaucratization, Usher (2002) points to five criticisms frequently made of the conventional PhD by thesis. The first is that it is too narrow and specialized. Second, it is not multi-disciplinary or even trans-disciplinary in its orientation. Third, it does not provide a broad enough set of skills to be acquired by the student. Fourth, it does not allow collaborative work. Finally, it separates itself off from industry and from industrial knowledge that provides the engine room for any successful economy. These criticisms treat PhD study as an homogenous experience with homogenous outputs, and also act to reify the university in the modern era. However, they have acted as drivers for recent interest round the world in reforming the PhD. We should be careful though, not to assume that this development in itself has been homogenous, not least in that reform of the PhD has gone hand in hand with the development of various new types of doctorate. For example, in the Canadian province of Ontario, the trend has been to reinvent and reconfigure the traditional PhD rather than launch a new type of professional doctorate (Allen *et al.* 2002).

One other point should be noted, which is that the original idea of creating a qualification for university teaching has become watered down in two ways. First, in the age of expansion of university provision, there were not enough university teachers in the UK with doctorates, or prepared to complete doctorates, to meet demand. Second, doctoral completion was tied much more closely to the needs of the economy as opposed to the specific needs of the university, and it was thought more appropriate for doctoral work to lead to specific forms of wealth creation. This move in turn led to the development of a particular type of doctoral degree, the professional doctorate, ironically reverting back to meeting the needs of the professions.

Changes in the doctorate

The period since the emergence of the first professional doctorate in the UK has been characterized by fundamental changes in higher education, and, in particular, in postgraduate provision. This is reflected in the rapid move from an elite to a mass higher education system (massification) and a consequent increase in the diversity of the student body (diversification) (Taylor 2002), leading to changes in the nature of the university (Dearing Report 1997; Barnett 1999; Jarvis 2000). In the UK, the postgraduate student body has grown from 26,700 postgraduates in 1961–62 to 448,700 in 2000–2001, of which 107,100 were research students; with no signs of a slow-down. This rapid development of higher education in the UK has inevitably led to renewed debates about the relationship of postgraduate education to employment, the relevance of higher education to professional work, the nature and structure of doctoral education (Becher *et al.* 1994; Delamont *et al.* 2000), and the purposes and agendas brought by students to their doctoral study. This is reflected in the publication of a number of government reports (for example the Harris Report 1996; the Dearing Report 1997) and an increased interest by bodies such as the Research Councils, HEFCE and QAA in research degrees.

This growing interest in the doctorate by external bodies has been due in large measure to the perceived inadequacies of the traditional PhD, both in terms of its usefulness and relevance and in terms of the length of time taken by students, in particular in the social science and arts fields, to complete the degree. As we have noted, part of this growing interest has been reflected in increasingly prescriptive requirements concerning the nature, amount, structure and outcomes of research training, which has as its purpose the development in its graduates of a range of generic and transferable skills related to employment.

Thus the Economic and Social Research Council includes in its latest Postgraduate Training Guidelines a clear statement about the need for research training programmes:

> A major emphasis in the Guidelines is on the provision of a broadly-based research training programme ... whilst a key element of the ESRC mission is to train postgraduates for careers in academic research it is recognised that not all postgraduates wish, or will be able, to pursue a career in academic research ... whatever career paths PhD graduates may follow, there are clear advantages to students if they have acquired general research skills and transferable employment-related skills.
>
> (ESRC 2001: 13)

This general commitment has been consolidated in the Joint Statement of The Research Councils and Arts and Humanities Research Board's *Skills Training Requirements for Research Students* (2002: 11), which aims to give a 'common view of the skills and experience of a typical research student'. These include the following:

A. **Research Skills and Techniques** – to be able to demonstrate:

- The ability to recognise and validate problems;
- An ability to summarise, document, report and reflect on progress.

B. **Research Environment** – to be able to:

- Understand relevant health and safety issues and demonstrate responsible working practices;
- Understand the processes for funding and evaluation of research.

C. **Research Management** – to be able to:

- Apply effective project management through the setting of research goals, intermediate milestones and prioritisation of activities;
- Use information technology appropriately for database management, recording and presenting information.

D. **Personal Effectiveness** – to be able to:

- Demonstrate a willingness and ability to learn and acquire knowledge;
- Demonstrate flexibility and open-mindedness;
- Demonstrate self-discipline, motivation and thoroughness;

- Recognise boundaries and draw upon/use sources of support as appropriate;
- Show initiative, work independently and be self-reliant.

E. **Communication Skills** – to be able to:

- Construct coherent arguments and articulate ideas clearly to a range of audiences, formally and informally through a range of techniques;
- Contribute to promoting the public understanding of one's research field;
- Effectively support the learning of others when involved in teaching, mentoring or demonstrating activities.

F. **Networking and Teamworking** – to be able to:

- Develop and maintain co-operative networks and working relationships with supervisors, colleagues and peers, within the institution and wider research community;
- Understand one's behaviours and impact on others when working in and contributing to the success of formal and informal teams;
- Listen, give and receive feedback and respond perceptively to others.

G. **Career Management** – to be able to:

- Appreciate the need for and show commitment to continued professional development;
- Take ownership for and manage one's own career progression, set realistic and achievable career goals, and identify and develop ways to improve employability;
- Demonstrate an insight into the transferable nature of research skills to other work environments and the range of career opportunities within and outside academia;
- Present one's skills, personal attributes and experiences through effective CVs, applications and interviews.

These extracts from the Joint Statement, presented here in some detail, demonstrate the extent to which pressure is being applied to the traditional doctorate (the PhD) to change direction, in order to become more relevant to the world of work and graduate employment.

A commitment to broader and transferable skills, often claimed to be 'employment related' has led to Research Council requirements for extensive and comprehensive training throughout the whole period of doctoral study, exemplified by initiatives such as the Research Student Log which enables students to take responsibility for auditing their skills, articulating training needs and recording the training undertaken in the course of their years of doctoral study. Thus the PhD itself is becoming 'professionalized', and to an extent acquiring some of the characteristics which have been developed as part of the professional doctorate. No longer seen as the individual pursuit of scholarship, for its own sake or as part of a lifetime interest, the PhD is now seen as a qualification which is required to develop clearly defined and marketable skills.

The most recent development within the UK in relation to the doctorate is an initiative of the Joint Funding Council (2003), which proposes minimum threshold standards that have to be met by universities before they are allowed to register research students. Under the heading *The Development of Research and Other Skills,* the document proposes a minimum threshold standard: 'Appropriate arrangements to be in place to help the student develop research and other skills'. In particular, the Joint Funding Council (2003: 7) suggests the following:

a) Student and supervisor or supervisory team to identify and agree a training needs analysis against the Research Councils' skills statement (*mentioned above*) as part of the induction process. Student training needs to be reviewed regularly.

b) Institution to provide the student with access to a training programme to develop research and other skills, as outlined in the Research Councils' skills statement.

c) Student to maintain a jointly agreed record of personal progress in the development of research and other skills.

d) Institution to formally review the training provided, to ensure that it is meeting the needs of its students.

e) Minimum level of activities defined and monitored to promote breadth and depth of knowledge and experience by means of the student's attendance at internal and external seminars, conferences and discussion forums, and participation in presentations, teaching and demonstrations.

The minimum threshold standards require universities to support students in explicit and generic skills training, and to ensure that the range of skills listed in the Joint Research Council statement is comprehensively covered. The idea of the original and lonely search for knowledge by the PhD student has become during the twenty-first century a highly formalized, bureaucratic and time-specific experience.

Models of doctoral study

The academy has always been associated with a form of pure knowledge-making. This distinguishes it from the application of this knowledge and indeed from the micro-politics of the knowledge industry where some forms of knowledge never have practical applications, or the market is so constructed that the product fails to find a buyer; or for other reasons. In this context, the PhD has always been the paradigm version of this form of knowledge. However, this suggests that applied knowledge and descriptions of application have not formed a part of the PhD experience. In this sense, we can identify a number of ideal models of doctorate study.

The first of these is the pure model referred to above. Model A has the following characteristics. It is located within the disciplinary arm of the university so that the subject matter of the thesis refers to an area of study that does not take one too far outside what is considered to be acceptable by gatekeepers to the discipline; and so that the way of approaching this subject matter may be acceptable to these gatekeepers (this would include epistemological orientation; methodological process, evaluative criteria, communicative desiderata; micro-political processes within the discipline and the like). This refers to the internal relations of the disciplinary arm of the university, and implies strong boundaries between itself and other disciplines within the academy; and strong boundaries between itself and other types of knowledge constructors, appliers and users. Furthermore, it implies strong and discrete boundaries between university departments and other bodies that may wish to regulate or control the academy's activity such as governmental or quasi-governmental agencies, generic university administrative bodies and the like. It implies a form of logocentrism and therefore of essentialism in that the university is seeking to protect a form of rationality that is particular to itself; indeed, it acts as the guardian to this type of discourse. It works by defending a variety of linguistic forms which preserve the logocentric nature of its discourse: the use of binary oppositions which marginalize some forms of life at the expense of others; the attachment of evaluative connotations to particular words or phrases; the alignment of some ideas with others; and the construction of boundaries round forms of thinking which act to exclude and marginalize. In short, it seeks to preserve insularity and elitism. Its intention is to influence the practicum in the long term and thus it has no desire to change practice in any immediate sense.

The second model has many of the features of our first; but it is beginning to embrace notions of trans-disciplinarity and looser boundaries between the disciplines, between itself *and* regulating bodies and other outside agencies. There is an acknowledgement that delineations between subjects or disciplines restrict the student in the development of original ideas about the subject matter. There is a further acknowledgement that ideas can only be understood within various contexts that are outside the university, so that the world out there certainly becomes the source for reflection about the world, and the arena for their deployment. This allows the possibility of developing models for the more effective delivery of the business of the workplace to which it is making reference. In particular, it sets itself in opposition to some of the perceived failings of the workplace, when these are understood as tradition, short-termism, the profit motive, performativity, de-theorization and hierarchy. It allows for the testing of ideas developed outside the university in the workplace setting, and the development of models of best practice. Furthermore, it is beginning to acknowledge that it has to engage with different logics of production in relation to knowledge; that its role is not purely a critical one in relation to how the professions work and how professionals function in the workplace.

The third is a servicing model, whereby the university and the doctoral student on behalf of the university abandons notions of universalizing truth, and adopts a more modest role in relation to society as a whole. This is where the student-practitioner devises a set of procedures developed from some acquaintance with the world of work that allows the practitioner to either better make sense of their workplace practice and/or develop new, original and more productive ways of working. This has some affinities with Reich's symbolic analysts, even if the language and conceptual frames used are developed outside the disciplinary arm of the university. Its mode of operation is as a commodity, and thus its value is decided in the marketplace.

These three models and hybrid versions of them are implicated in the various types of doctorates being developed. Reflecting the pressures for diversity in postgraduate education in the UK, the traditional doctorate, the PhD, has in recent years been supplemented by four other 'types' of doctorate: the practice-based doctorate, professional doctorates, the New Route PhD and PhD by publication, of which the professional doctorate is the most substantial and significant development. Thus this 15-year period of gradual 'professionalization' of the traditional doctorate (PhD) coincided with the development in the UK of a new form of doctorate, the professional doctorate, which emerged in response to the needs of universities to expand student numbers and to diversify programmes, the needs of practitioners for higher forms of professional development, the needs of some professions for higher level qualifications, and the greater legitimacy accorded to workplace learning and workplace-generated knowledge. In the next chapter we trace its history and development.

3

The Evolution of Professional Doctorates

Introduction

The professional doctorate was introduced to the UK in the 1990s (Bourner *et al.* 2001a). In the past ten or so years, this degree has becoming increasingly popular, and this is reflected in the growing number of universities that are offering the degree in an increasing range of professional fields, and in the ever increasing number of students who have graduated. There are a number of factors that appear to have influenced the evolution of the professional doctorate. These include developments in Higher Education and in particular doctorate education, and more importantly, changing relationships between university and employment cultures, both in the UK and across the world.

Although it is difficult to produce a general definition of a professional doctorate, the UK Council for Graduate Education Report suggests that:

> the professional doctorate is a further development of the taught doctorate . . . but the field of study is a professional discipline, rather than academic enquiry and scholarship . . . most professional doctorates are designed to meet a particular professional need . . . the research element of a professional doctorate is focussed on professional practice . . . it is possible for the work to make an original contribution to the way in which theory is applied, or to the nature of practice within a profession.
>
> (2002: 7)

The defining feature of the professional doctorate is a focus on professional work, reflecting a recognition that work-based learning should be extended to the highest level of award, the doctorate. An earlier report by the same body for example, suggested that:

> the aim of the 'professional doctorate' is the personal development of the candidate coupled with the advancement of the subject or the

profession. They include a substantial taught component and one or more practice-based research projects which result in the submission of a thesis or portfolio of projects which has to be defended by oral examination. The degrees are equivalent in standard to the PhD but different in their approach to the achievement of 'doctorateness'.

(UKCGE 1998: 6)

Again, a defining feature is a focus on the development of the individual in relation to their professional work.

Professional doctorates appear to have a number of elements in common: taught courses, specification of learning outcomes often in the form of employment related skills, cohort-based pedagogies, and usually a reduced thesis length in comparison with the PhD thesis, but with the same requirement for originality. However, as we suggested above, the increasingly prescriptive requirements of the PhD within the social sciences, and the recent introduction of the so-called 1+3 (first year MRes plus 3 years PhD) by the ESRC is bringing the PhD more into line with professional doctorates by introducing substantial taught elements, and by requiring the development of key transferable and employment-related skills.

The Quality Assurance Agency Framework for Higher Education Qualifications (QAA 2001) places both PhD and 'other doctorates' at level 5; professional doctorates are given a clear 'credit rating' in the Credit and HE qualifications guidelines. Although a number of professional doctorates have stated credit ratings, they are not (yet) widely used, and there is relatively little experience of APL/APEL (Accreditation of Prior Learning/Accreditation of Prior Experiential Learning). The qualification descriptors for qualifications at doctoral level provide an impetus both to define the outcomes of doctoral study and to make these professionally relevant. Doctorates are awarded to students who have demonstrated:

i.   The creation and interpretation of new knowledge, through original research, or other advanced scholarship, of a quality to satisfy peer review, extend the forefront of the discipline, and merit publication;

ii. A systematic acquisition and understanding of a substantial body of knowledge which is at the forefront of an academic discipline or area of professional practice;

iii. The general ability to conceptualize, design and implement a project for the generation of new knowledge, applications or understanding at the forefront of the discipline, and to adjust the project design in the light of unforeseen problems;

iv. A detailed understanding of applicable techniques for research and advanced academic enquiry.

Typically, holders of the qualification will be able to:

a.   Make informed judgements on complex issues . . .

b.   Continue to undertake pure and/or applied research

and will have:

> c. The qualities and transferable skills necessary for employment requiring the exercise of personal responsibility and largely autonomous initiative in complex and unpredictable situations, in professional or equivalent environments.
>
> (QAA 2001: 8)

The timing of the introduction of professional doctorates coincides with requirements by bodies such as the QAA that degree programmes are accompanied by explicit learning outcomes, and it is clear from professional doctorate prospectuses that the majority of professional doctorates provide clear learning outcomes, both for the degree as a whole and for the individual courses which make up the programme.

In a more general sense, the QAA Framework raises particular issues for the PhD, which are foregrounded by the emergence of professional doctorates. A major issue is parity of level (and assessment) of the professional doctorate in relation to the PhD, and the potentially different notions of 'doctorateness' embodied in the two forms of doctorate. UK professional doctorate regulations suggest that they have parity with the PhD and make the same requirement for 'originality', though this is usually defined in terms of application of knowledge or contribution to the professional field. A second issue is the curriculum model that has been adopted – the specification of learning outcomes – and the related issue of identifying a professional doctorate product that enables assessment of these intended learning outcomes. This is in comparison with the assessment of the PhD, which has no stated learning outcomes, and is assessed almost entirely through a single thesis. Typically, professional doctorates require students to complete a thesis, which is assessed in the same way as a PhD thesis, usually by viva. The final 'ability' listed in the QAA descriptors fits the professional doctorate and articulates aspirations held by many professional doctorate programme directors:

> Holders of the qualification will have the qualities and transferable skills necessary for employment requiring the exercise of personal responsibility and largely autonomous initiative in complex and unpredictable situations, in professional or equivalent environments.
>
> (QAA 2001: 8)

It is difficult to see how the traditional PhD enables its graduates to have these qualities, although the Joint Research Councils statement and the Joint Funding Councils' minimum threshold standards may go a long way to achieving this in the future.

International context

The professional doctorate appears to have developed in this form in anglophone countries such as North America and subsequently Australia, and later the UK. It is unclear how far this form of professionally focussed doctorate will extend to other European university systems, though the extension of *The Bologna Process* to doctoral level degrees predicted for the Berlin summit in 2003 will clearly bring pressures for greater convergence of systems at the degree level where the PhD already had international currency.

In Canada, 'the EdD arose in response to a demand by nineteenth century educational practitioners to further their professional education' (Allen *et al.* 2002: 205). The EdD programme was established at the University of Toronto as early as 1894, predating the establishment of the PhD in that university. However, as Allen *et al.* suggest:

> professional doctoral degrees have never enjoyed widespread popularity in Canada . . . and many professional schools and faculties are choosing to develop or redesign PhD programs to meet the needs of the field over the creation of separate professional doctorates . . . after almost a century of existence, the future of the EdD is unclear, as the past five years have witnessed a steady decline in its enrolment.
>
> (2002: 205)

Indeed, a number of professional doctorates have already been discontinued, while the university redesigns the PhD with a greater focus on the integration of theory and practice, and the creation of more flexibility.

In the USA, the first Doctor of Education (EdD) degree was introduced at Harvard University in 1921. The EdD, and indeed other professional doctorates in the USA have tended to be conceived of as a 'pre-service award rather than an in-service award for advanced professional development' (Bourner *et al.* 2000b: 9), and have been developed both in universities and in professional schools, for example, schools of psychology. Although the PhD degree in the USA usually includes substantial coursework and examination, which is assessed together with a research-based dissertation, professional doctorates frequently include both greater amounts of coursework, shorter dissertations and periods of internship or practice.

The first professional doctorate was established much later in Australia with the Doctor of Creative Arts at Wollongong in 1984, followed by the Doctorate in Legal/Juridical Science in 1989. The first EdD in Australia appeared at around the same time as it appeared in Britain, with the EdD in 1990 at the University of Melbourne. Bowden *et al.* (2002: 20) suggest that, 'the 1990s was the decade when professional doctorates came both to England (Bourner *et al.* 2001a), and Australia (Trigwell *et al.* 1997)'. By 1996 professional doctorates were available in education, business, law, psychology, health sciences, humanities, design and architecture (Poole and Spear 1997), and were offered as 'an in-service or professional development award, concerned with production of knowledge in the professions' (Maxwell and Shanahan 1997: 133), in contrast to the pre-service professional doctorate of the USA.

Since their introduction in the 1990s, there has been considerable interest in professional doctorates in Australia, where biennial conferences on professional doctorates have been held since 1996. Maxwell (2003b) draws a distinction between 'first' and 'second' generation professional doctorates that merits exploration. He suggests that 'first generation' professional doctorates mostly follow the 'coursework plus thesis model and appear to be dominated by academe' (279), and are characterized as only structurally different from the PhD. The 'second generation' of professional doctorate, on the other hand, according to Seddon is characterized by a shift in orientation of both site and nature of knowledge production:

> (The) trajectory, from a substantially taught professional doctorate depending heavily on coursework and individualised supervision, towards a learning environment that provides diverse support to facilitate learning by doctoral students (and staff) is what I understand to be the move from first to second generation professional Doctorates.
>
> (2000: 3)

This shift from 'first' to 'second generation' may be seen as a key step in the evolution of the professional doctorate; that is a move from a doctorate dominated in form and structure by the academy, where academic knowledge is privileged over professional knowledge, to one that embraces the complexity and challenge of new knowledge production in partnership with the workplace and which empowers practitioners to develop their professional practice in a mode which may be very different from the traditional thesis. An example of this cited by Maxwell (2003b: 284) is the EdD at the University of Western Sydney which aims to develop a 'partnership between the university and the employer so that doctoral degree experiences are integrated with the needs of the employer'; the research 'product' is a portfolio which contains at least six pieces 'of which four need to be published, conference presentations, or those placed on the internet'. In this way the student 'output' is produced in a format and style to which practitioners are more accustomed, relevant to their employment, and without the shift of discourse and conceptualization frequently demanded by the more academic format of the thesis. Here the site for professional doctoral activity is the intersection of the profession, the workplace and the university (Lee *et al.* 2000).

Historical development of professional doctorates in the UK

The first professional doctorate in the UK was in clinical psychology which was proposed in 1987 and emerged as the first DClinPsy in 1989 (Donn *et al.* 2000). However, this development was a 'pre-service' doctorate and was part of a wider initiative of credentialing, licensing to practise and establishing professional status for clinical psychologists, largely within the National Health Service (see Chapter 10). The professional doctorate in clinical psychology evolved historically from a desire for accreditation for clinical psychologists and acquiring the licence to practice within the National Health Service; thus the original Diploma qualification became a Master's level qualification, and in turn, this qualification acquired doctoral level status, in response to demands by the profession both for extended training and for higher status. More recently, university psychology departments have developed 'in-service' clinical psychology doctorates that are intended for qualified clinical psychologists in mid-career who seek a high level continuing professional development programme, though this may also be related to issues of status and parity within the NHS (see Chapter 10).

As in Australia, a key impetus for the development of the professional doctorate was a concern that the 'traditional' doctorate, the PhD, was primarily a preparation for an academic career, and did not meet the needs of practitioners or practising professionals. It was also suggested that there was a 'need for a research-based approach to deal with some of the complex problems faced by various professions' (UKCGE 2002: 34) in the increasingly complex world of work. Thus the Government's 1993 White Paper on Research Policy (Office of Science and Technology 1993: 3) stated that 'the traditional PhD is not well-matched to the needs of careers outside research in academic or an industrial research laboratory'; this concern has already led to changes in the PhD itself. Alongside this concern were a number of other factors, which influenced the development of professional doctorates; and these included:

- Universities expanding their provision to respond to external demands and pressures, to increase their student numbers and therefore university funding, a general expansion of higher education and consequential qualification 'inflation';
- The pace of change in the workplace and work activity becoming more complex and requiring higher level qualifications;
- Professions and professionals embracing 'evidence-based' practice, the development of the concept of the 'reflective practitioner' and the extension of professional development requirements;
- The development of Work-Based Learning, and the increasing acceptance within universities of the legitimacy of knowledge production in the workplace.

The first UK 'in-service' professional doctorates for experienced professionals were established in the early 1990s in the fields of education, engineering and business administration. Since that time a wide range of professional doctorates have been developed in different professional fields, and by 1999 professional doctorates could be found in 25 fields (Bourner *et al.* 2000b; 2001a; 2001b). More recently, universities have extended the degree to an increasingly wide range of professional fields, from medical areas such as pharmacy, nursing, public health, veterinary medicine, dental science, to social work, and arts-based fields such as architecture, fine art, musical arts, musical composition and the broad field of psychology and psychotherapy. There is also a generic professional doctorate in work-based learning, offered by the University of Middlesex, which provides the opportunity for members of different professional groups to work together and focus on generic work-based issues.

It is perhaps significant that the two fields which first embraced the professional doctorate in the UK in 1992 – education and engineering – appear to have done so for different reasons. According to the UKCGE (2002: 19), 'the Engineering Doctorate resulted from the perceived need to have a high status route for young engineers to enter industrial careers, with a combination of a high level of technical expertise and well-developed skills in problem-solving and team working. It was intended to operate in full-time mode, and be aimed at recent graduates.' The EngD was initiated by the Engineering and Physical Sciences Research Council (EPSRC) which provided the rationale, framework and funding for the EngD (see below). This 'top-down' initiative has resulted in a clear identity of EngD programmes, reflected in a clear purpose and outcome for participants, or research engineers.

The EdD, on the other hand, 'has developed to bring a demonstrably high level of research enquiry to bear within a practical context. This route is particularly relevant for experienced education professionals and is almost invariably undertaken on a part-time basis' (UKCGE 2002: 19). EdD programmes have been developed through the initiative of universities themselves and without the support of a professional body or a research council, possibly because the field of education is professionally diffuse, and has hitherto lacked one professional body or a clear professional identity.

Other professional doctorates have developed within the UK in response to pressure from the relevant profession; for example professional doctorates in social work and nursing, as part of an increasing status of qualification, or as part of an offer of high level professional development, or as part of a commitment to research and learning on the part of the profession. A clear example of pressure from the profession comes again from the British Psychological Society (the BPS) which has responsibility for accrediting professional qualifications and for setting standards of entry to the profession; the BPS has a role in the accreditation of pre-service or initial qualification doctorates in clinical psychology, and has increasingly become involved in setting standards for the in-service doctorate in clinical psychology (for experienced practitioners).

The current trend of new professional doctorates appears likely to continue for the foreseeable future. However, with changes to the PhD, and a clear 'professionalization' of that degree, it seems likely that universities will bring the doctorates closer into line with each other. While the relevant Research Council (EPSRC) has a clear role in defining the framework and the quality standard for the EngD, the ESRC included professional doctorates in its most recent Recognition Exercise and welcomed their development:

> The ESRC welcomes the development of professional doctorate programmes, some of which are also known as 'taught' doctorates, and the potential they have to enable students to more directly apply academic

knowledge and training. Being more applied than the 'traditional' PhD, they are particularly relevant and attractive to practitioners, notably in subjects such as management and business studies and education. However, there is currently much variability in terms of expectations, content and level.

(ESRC 2001: 79)

At the present time, ESRC recognition of professional doctorates serves as a 'kitemark' for the particular degree, though this may serve also to provide a benchmark or framework for the development of particular features of the professional doctorate. Given the gradual changes in the nature of the doctorate within the university, the requirements by external bodies that the doctorate lead to a range of transferable skills, and by the QAA that there be specific learning outcomes, there appears to be a clear role for either a Research Council or a professional body, or both, in the creation of a more common understanding of the nature, the purpose, the outcomes and the assessment of the professional doctorate. The Association of Business Schools, although neither a Research Council nor a professional body, has taken a clear initiative in relation to this for the DBA.

The business doctorate

The DBA emerged in the early 1990s in the UK as a progression from the popular and successful MBA degree. Universities saw the opportunity for expansion, and MBA graduates welcomed the opportunity for progression, and for further professional development. In the same way that the MBA was tailored to a specific segment of the market in contrast to the more generic framing of the traditional Masters programme, the DBA likewise was designed for a specialized part of the market in contrast to the traditional PhD. The DBA programme expanded rapidly across universities, and by 1999 there were DBA programmes in 16 universities in the UK. In 1997 the Association of Business Schools responded to the growing variety in DBA programmes by developing guidelines.

The Association of Business Schools (ABS) is a self-funding charity which brings together 102 of the leading business schools in the UK and which has developed *Guidelines for the Doctor of Business Administration Degree (DBA)* (1998: 3) 'in response to requests from members of ABS who see benefits to themselves and the market place in attempting to reach consensus and then publicly clarify the nature of the DBA and how it differs from other qualifications and particularly the PhD'. These guidelines define the DBA as:

primarily designed to enable a significant contribution to the enhancement of professional practice in the business area through the application and development of theoretical frameworks ... a professional practice doctorate and ... concerned with researching real business and managerial issues via the critical review and systematic application of appropriate theories and research to professional practice . . . intended to provide opportunity for considerable personal development, such that the participant achieves a greater level of effectiveness as a professional practitioner or manager . . . equal in status and rigour to the PhD.

(ABS 1998: 3)

One programme claims that the DBA:

takes you on to a greater contribution in the workplace . . . the outcome of the research is designed to contribute to the management approach, the thinking or processes of the sponsoring organisation . . . the DBA will help you to develop a multiple perspectives approach to considering managerial problems or issues, a critical appreciation of your own insights and conclusions, the ability to undertake rigorous management research, the ability to reflect and build on your own learning.

(ABS 1998: 3)

Bourner *et al.* (2000a) analysed the programme structures, content, and learning support and identified a wide range of DBA structure and content of programme, while Bareham and Bourner (2000) analysed programmes for their learning outcomes, which tended to cover three categories: research, personal development, knowledge of business and management. They identified the following learning outcomes of the DBA:

1. Research

- An appreciation of the potential contribution of research to the work of senior managers;
- The capacity to plan and carry out a research project in the field of business administration;
- The capacity to make an original contribution to knowledge of practice in the field of business management;
- The capacity to implement research findings in terms of management practice within an organisation.

2. Personal Development

- The capacity to plan and manage own learning and continuing professional development;
- The skill of improving own performance through reflection on past practice.

3. Knowledge of Business and Management

- Knowledge and understanding of business and management to at least the level of a masters degree in the field of study.

(Bareham and Bourner 2000: 395)

These learning outcomes map clearly onto both QAA level descriptors and the statement of research and employment-related skills drawn up by the Research Councils and endorsed by the Funding Councils.

Ruggeri-Stevens *et al.* (2001) considered the issue of assessment standards, and concluded that there remained a tension between the PhD and the DBA in terms of the definition of 'doctorateness', and in particular the mode of assessment that would enable evaluation of this broad range of learning outcomes. In particular they highlighted some problems in the assessment of the DBA:

a) The career focus in most DBA prospectuses was senior manager rather than academic. In view of this it seems strange that the assessment requirements . . . focussed so tightly on the capacity to make an original contribution to the body of knowledge of practice in business/management rather than the ability to manage.

b) Despite the espoused learning outcomes . . . it is not clear where, how or indeed whether, the reflective practitioner component of most DBA courses was being assessed.

c) Particularly at the point of final assessment the thesis appeared to carry the evidence of the DBA candidate's achievement of a wider range of learning outcomes than that found on most PhD programmes.

(2001: 70)

This resonates with the experience of programme directors of the education doctorate.

The education doctorate

The first Doctorate in Education (EdD) programme in the UK was introduced by the University of Bristol in 1992. Ten years later the EdD is offered in almost 40 universities and shows no sign of a reduction in popularity. The EdD developed in the UK in response to a need of education professionals for a higher form of professional development. Thus, the PhD was not thought to meet the needs of professionals who had taken a Masters degree in education and who wished to pursue research within their professional field. In the early stages of the development of the programme, there was some confusion over whether the EdD was a 'taught' doctorate, and therefore both easier to obtain and of second-class status in comparison with the PhD. Most universities rapidly discovered that neither of these was the case. Some university departments of education showed resistance to the development of the EdD, aware that there were many practitioners studying for the PhD and that education PhDs were frequently practice- or work-based. However, the success and demand of early programmes, and the model provided by other countries, in particular Australia, ensured the spread of the EdD, first among pre-1992 universities, and more recently in post-1992 universities.

The EdD is a professionally focussed doctorate for education professionals where experienced professionals or practitioners develop research skills, reflect rigorously on their practice and carry out a substantial piece of research. Some examples from prospectuses of the target or purpose of the EdD are:

> The degree is aimed at experienced professionals in education who wish to extend their professional expertise and training, while not intending to become career researchers.

> The EdD is a rigorous research-based and research-driven qualification focused on the improvement of professional practice.

> The overall aim of the degree is to produce people who are skilled consumers, evaluators, commissioners and producers of research.

> Senior education professionals today have to work in an environment which relies increasingly on sophisticated knowledge and expertise in research.

The field of education is professionally diffuse and EdD programmes reflect this in their student participation: school, college and university teachers from all phases of education (pre-school, primary, secondary, post-compulsory and higher education), and all stages of seniority (main grade teachers and lecturers to head teachers and principals), administrators in education and in local authorities, related professionals from medically related fields or other professional fields, and international organizations. Like the DBA, the EdD is covered by the ESRC as its Research Council, and a significant number of EdD programmes sought and gained ESRC recognition in the 2001 Recognition Exercise. However, unlike the DBA, the EdD has no body that has taken a professional overview or provided a framework or standards for the EdD, and there is considerable diversity between the programmes. Over the past five years there has been a forum for directors of EdD programmes, based at the Institute of Education, University of London; this is an informal network which meets annually and where programme directors are able to share good practice and raise issues. In the absence of another body to develop an overview or a framework for EdD programmes, the network has provided a useful opportunity for issues to be explored, perspectives to be developed, and information to be exchanged.

Most of the EdD programmes in the UK are part-time and last between three and seven years. Like other professional doctorates, they tend to have a modular structure, many are credit rated, and most of them have clearly stated learning outcomes, many of which are related to professional work and employment. Like the DBA, EdD programmes require the submission of a research-based thesis as the final product of the doctorate; this is assessed in ways similar to the assessment of the PhD, thus raising some of the same issues as with the DBA.

The engineering doctorate

The EngD was also first offered in this country in 1992 and was initiated by the Engineering and Physical Sciences Research Council (EPSRC), in response to the recommendations of the Parnaby Report, as a:

> radical alternative to the traditional PhD, being better suited to the needs of industry, and providing a more vocationally oriented doctorate in engineering ... designed to provide engineers with business and technical competencies by applying new knowledge to industrially relevant doctoral research, employing the skills gained from an intensive programme of taught coursework.
>
> (EPSRC website)

Unlike the EdD, and more similar to the DBA, the EngD may be seen as a natural progression from the MEng, a four-year integrated Masters degree created in the 1980s as a result of the Finniston Report *Engineering our Future* (1980). This report coined the word 'formation' to describe the broader needs of engineering education to include not only business and management topics but also increased professional skills, and it was designed to produce graduates who had acquired specific capabilities and competencies as well as knowledge.

The EPSRC took a 'top down' approach to the EngD, issuing Best Practice Guidelines, which aim to ensure the quality and standard of the programmes. Their stated aim is to:

- Provide REs (research engineers, the name given to students on EngD programmes) with experience of rigorous, leading edge research in a business context;
- Develop competencies which equip REs for a range of roles in industry;
- Provide a mechanism and framework for high quality collaboration between academic groups and a range of companies;
- Contribute to the body of knowledge on a particular discipline, industrial sector or multidisciplinary theme.

(EPSRC website)

This is the most clearly articulated statement of purpose of a professional doctorate. It is significant that EngD programmes were initiated by and have developed with the strong support, including funding, of the Research Council (the EPSRC). The statement of purpose is followed by a clear statement of the competencies to be achieved which include: 'expert knowledge, an appreciation of ... engineering culture, project and programme management skills, teamwork and leadership skills, communication skills, the ability to apply skills/knowledge to new and unusual situations, the ability to seek optimal solutions to complex and multifaceted problems' (EPSRC website), a list not dissimilar from that produced in the Joint Statement of the Research Councils and the AHRB (Arts and Humanities Research Board).

These competencies are clearly intended to meet the requirements of the world of work outside the academy.

The first EngD programmes started in 1992, funded by EPSRC as a 'pilot', in five 'Centres', for which universities had been invited to bid, following inception of the scheme. A Centre consists of one or more university departments and a number of sponsoring industrial companies, and provides the overall co-ordination of the programme. The scheme was reviewed formally in 1997 (EPSRC 1997) with a recommendation for expansion to further Centres. The Review concluded that:

> the EngD shows every prospect of producing graduates capable of becoming future managers of research and being the innovators of the future . . . the 'Centre' approach to management of the EngD is essential to the provision of the training and to facilitate the industry/academic interactions required for a successful programme . . . the EngD is seen as a superb way for universities and industry to work together.
>
> (EPSRC 1997)

Universities are invited to apply to the EPSRC for funding to set up an EngD Centre, based in the lead university, and run by a Centre Director assisted by academic and industrial supervisors. The Centre may become a 'hub of interaction between different schools within the university and between the university and participating companies' (EPSRC Website, Winter 2002–03).

It is clear that the Review emphasized the importance of the concept of 'Centre' and defined an 'Ideal Centre' as one that would:

- Be associated with a university department or departments which can demonstrate high quality teaching and an excellent research base relevant to the theme or focus of the projects;
- Focus on a particular technical discipline, inter-disciplinary topic or industrial sector;
- Encourage a range of companies to participate, with no one company sponsoring more that 25% of the EPSRC supported population of Research Engineers (REs) at the Centre;
- Report to EPSRC every two years for assessment purposes;
- Use a formal credit system for taught elements;
- Ensure that the timing of training optimises the balance between the company requirements to build the collaboration early in the programme and the provision of necessary skills and competencies in good time for them to be applied;
- Have supervisory arrangements which reflect the breadth of projects, including management, financial or other expertise as appropriate;
- Ensure the framework for the programme includes: REs arranging regular academic/industrial supervisor meetings, REs being expected to spend 40–60% of their time in the company, a clear problem resolution process, publication of research in refereed journals, mechanisms for REs to take courses elsewhere when appropriate;

- Monitor the progress of both RE and project throughout the programme and encourage REs to log personal and professional progress, plan towards Chartered status of graduates, hold a mid-term review of the progress of the RE on the project;
- Track the career progression of graduates for a further review in 5 years' time.

(EPSRC 1997)

The EPSRC also co-ordinates annual meetings of Co-ordinators of Centres in order to share best practice.

Following the Review of 1997, the scheme was extended and a further five centres started in 1999, followed by a further five in 2001, so that the EngD is now offered at 15 centres, most of which specialize in aerospace, transport knowledge and systems engineering, environmental technology, steel technology and manufacturing systems engineering. The EngD provides an example of a professional doctorate set up by a Research Council and with an explicit role in response to a number of government reports critical of the role of the PhD in relation to industry. The clear direction provided by the EPSRC, the funding available to Centres to attract Research Engineers, the five-year review and subsequent Best Practice Notes, the annual meeting of Centre Directors, all contribute to a clear identity for the engineering profession and the research engineers undertaking the EngD.

Conclusion

At a time of expansion of student numbers and the development of university programmes to meet this demand, both the PhD and the professional doctorate are under pressure to change. Although there are variations in practice within the PhD, and its assessment is by no means robust, its structure and the criteria of originality are widespread and widely understood. The professional doctorate is much less well understood, and there are a range of stakeholders (for example Research Councils, professional bodies, other co-ordinating bodies such as the ABS) developing views on it, with some aspects in common and others discipline or profession specific. This means that there continues to be some ignorance both in the university and the professional community as to the nature of the professional doctorate. Despite the initiative of bodies such as the UKCGE, professional doctorates are being developed without reference to a wider framework for the professional doctorate. This raises the question as to how far there is a 'generic' professional doctorate and how far it is profession specific?

Initiatives by external bodies such as the Research Councils, the Higher Education Funding Councils (HEFCE, HEFCW, SHEFC), and the QAA are resulting in changes to the PhD in the UK and are requiring universities to 'professionalize' the doctorate. The specification of skills and competencies of the PhD and the requirement for learning outcomes of the doctorate are contributing to a substantial change to the way in which the PhD has been conceptualized and organized. These requirements have brought the PhD closer in structure and conceptualization to the professional doctorate. In Toronto, Canada, at least, this has resulted in universities making the PhD more flexible and closing EdD programmes because of reduced student take-up.

Yet, a defining feature of the professional doctorate is its focus on professional life and work, and an encouragement for participants to enhance their professional work through undertaking doctoral level study which privileges professional knowledge. In the UK at least, professional doctorates do not appear to be giving way to a more flexible and revitalized PhD programme, and clearly programmes such as the EngD fulfil a complementary role to the PhD within the engineering profession.

The EngD provides a model for the integration of academic work with professional work or the role of work-based learning within the academy. This integration is clearly enhanced by the structure and organization of the EngD, and in particular the overall co-ordination by the EngD Centre, which brings together professionals from the university with those in industry. This is facilitated both by the funding and framework provided by the EPSRC, and by the employability of the research engineers, who are frequently taken on for employment by the sponsoring industry. The link is further facilitated by the assessment of the EngD in which both academic and industry staff participate and which frequently involves a portfolio of projects rather than one traditional academic thesis. For other professional doctorates (for example, the DBA and the EdD) the link between theory and practice or between academic work and professional work is more difficult to develop, and almost all require the submission of a major research-based thesis as the final 'product'. This is assessed using mainly academic criteria and it makes integration more difficult.

As university education expands further with a consequent expansion of postgraduate and doctoral provision, it appears likely that there will be increased guidance provided by external agencies, with increased requirement for credit ratings, accreditation of prior learning and more flexible structures which meet the needs of an increasingly diverse student body. This chapter has provided an overview of the evolution of the professional doctorate within the UK over the past ten or so years since its introduction to the UK in 1992. The next chapter examines some of these ideas in practice, where the practices are the student-practitioner's academic and workplace settings. Given the inherent complexity of day-to-day life and its refusal neatly to conform to theoretical models, a note of caution is in order here. Below we develop a fourfold model of knowledge modes: disciplinarity, technical rationality, dispositionality and criticality. However, it would be perverse to insist that students, lecturers, departments, programmes and even institutions fit easily into them. In other words, we cannot read off in an unproblematic way what individuals actually do from the theoretical schema that we offer. What this process does allow us to do is develop a set of signposts to begin to make sense of the complicated lives of student-practitioners engaging in higher doctorate study.

Part 2

Knowledge Matters

4

Academic and Professional Knowledge

Introduction

Gibbons *et al.*'s (1994) well-known typology of knowledge modes rests on a bifurcated distinction between disciplinary knowledge constructed in the university and trans-disciplinary knowledge produced outside the university. Mode 1 knowledge is understood as linear, causal and cumulative, as originating in universities and other research institutes, as applied to solve practical problems outside the university, as 'closed' in that the source for knowledge always originates from within the discipline, as reductionist, and as determinant of what counts as significant in society. Gibbons *et al.* contrast this with Mode 2 knowledge which has four characteristics: instead of science preceding technology, technology is seen as autonomous and able to develop outside of science; it is trans-disciplinary with the source for identifying problems and solutions resting in the practice setting; it is synoptic rather than reductionist with an emphasis on the whole process of innovation; and it is heterarchical and transient. Mode 2 knowledge is not understood as a replacement for Mode 1 knowledge, but as an alternative, and the tensions between the two types leads to various hybrid forms of knowledge which have found one of their expressions in the development of professional doctorates.

This narrative, as Lee (1999) makes clear, is beset with problems. Its characterization of the university as disciplinary, heterogeneous, hierarchical, form-preserving and scientist (Habermas 1987) is outmoded and ideal. Professional doctorates in the UK, one manifestation of the production of knowledge, are underpinned by different epistemologies, different strengths of disciplinary boundaries, different understandings of the relationship between theoretical and practical knowledge and different ways of operationalizing these constructs in the development of their programmes. Though there are undoubted tensions between the different sites of knowledge production, the bifurcated model developed by Gibbons *et al.* fails to take account of practices that are trans-disciplinary, practicum-sourced, hierarchical and form-preserving. Furthermore, within the professional doctorate itself, knowledge may originate from and within the professional practice, and yet the solution for the practitioner (controlled and ultimately validated by the university as disciplinary knowledge) may be found within the disciplinary practice.

This chapter will focus on the way these professional doctorates construct both knowledge itself and the act of doing research. In part, this is through specific research training courses provided by the university for doctoral study. However, more fundamentally, it is through the way universities understand and in the process construct relationships between academic and professional knowledge. Four modes of knowledge can be identified.

Mode 1: Disciplinary knowledge

Knowledge-construction of this type involves the student in being inducted into a disciplinary practice that is well established in the university. The student, if they are successful in the practice, engages in a form of self-examination which Barnett (1997: 97) describes as 'self-reflection on the student's own disciplinary competence'. This involves the student in reflecting on those theoretical and methodological frameworks through which they understand reality and more closely aligning themselves with those which characterize their chosen discipline or sub-discipline. The rules of the discipline, in this ideal model, are based on a set of criteria for evaluating knowledge, a set of definitional criteria which includes and excludes what is considered proper knowledge, and a set of methodological criteria through which an initiate operates – a set of procedures which delineates a practitioner from a non-practitioner. An indifference is shown to other forms of practice, whether they be other disciplines or the practice setting. The practice setting is the source for theoretical deliberation, but the discipline retains its role as the ultimate arbiter of knowledge claims; those knowledge claims being classificatory, evaluative and methodological. A disciplinary practice changes over time because some players in the game are substituted for others, and because the rules of the game develop and evolve. These rules may be invisible and tacit or formally codified and explicit. Success is achieved when those rules are internalized and the student is initiated into the discipline.

The picture is, however, more complicated. First, disciplinary practices are to a greater or lesser extent closed with strong or weak boundaries between them and other forms of knowledge. Of the three types of professional doctorate that were examined, each displayed different characteristics as disciplinary practices. The EngD recruited students with little prior experience of the workplace, was staffed in general by members of the faculty with industrial experience, was characterized by a view of knowledge which was linear and non-contested, and, though influenced by developments in the physical sciences, drew robust boundaries between itself and other disciplines.

Furthermore, the engineering discipline understood itself as a practical activity, with the end product as outputs that were able to compete in the marketplace. The DBA had weaker boundaries between itself and other disciplines, was more fragmented as a discipline, adopted within itself a less coherent view of knowledge and displayed conflicting attitudes towards the practice setting. At the other extreme to the EngD, the EdD recruited experienced professionals, displayed itself as fragmented with a number of sub-disciplines emerging, and generally was preoccupied with boundary maintenance and sustenance.

Second, the extent to which students are inducted into these formations of knowledge depends to some degree on the student themselves and on the area in which they work. Many students displayed a form of strategic compliance with the demands of the discipline, especially as they are manifested in the final examination, or entry point to the discipline. Frequently, the student fabricated entry to the discipline (cf. Ball 2001), and therefore to the practice, by pretending to conform to its demands; when in reality the requisite amount of emotional and intellectual attachment to the discipline was simply not present. An EdD student comments on their viva voce examination:

> And he seemed to concentrate mainly on my methodology. And he felt, I had to actually make some amendments. I used grounded theory and concentrated on Strauss and Corbin. And I had not mentioned Glazer any more, and he wanted me to include some things on Glazer, and it took me ages to just find something that was quite recent until I found out he wrote his own little monograph and had founded his own press. That's why I couldn't find it anywhere, and, well, it was quite interesting to read. But I still would not really follow his directions. But I had to include at least some things, probably why I hadn't followed that direction. And, so that was his pet area then in the viva? He even insisted, he said himself, and he sent me an email a bit later. I thought that was quite a bit cheeky, and he said, 'I want a reference from Glazer's latest publication.' So, it seemed to take up most of the viva. And his second point was why I hadn't related what I'd found or what I was discussing to the North American situation. And I felt, 'well, I didn't set out to do this'. I set out to [do something different], so I had to do it, and then I realised, he had written quite a bit about the North American situation on professionalism and teachers, so I had a look at this, and that was the second amendment.

For the student the knowledge that is being demanded is esoteric and irrelevant. For the examiner, or disciplinary gatekeeper, it is central to the practice.

Disciplinary knowledge, as it is manifested in professional doctorates, may also be expressed generically; that is, though it displays two of our three characteristics of disciplinarity: an indifference to the practice setting and the designation of the practice setting as merely the source for theoretical deliberation, it shares a common purpose with other disciplines located in the academy. Rather than being concerned with outcomes or performativity, traditional university and cross-disciplinary agendas are pursued, so that broadly the purpose is to defend notions of truth, objectivity and dispassionate study. Again, the disciplinary practices of the three professional doctorates being examined displayed different characteristics in relation to this, with the EngD being characterized by agreed and settled views on what constitutes good practice and how it can be known, and the DBA and the EdD less sure of their epistemological foundations.

This generic form of knowledge, displayed in its most robust form on the EngD, may be construed as 'scientistic' (Habermas 1974: 4), where scientific description is understood as the only possible way of seeing the world: it refers to 'science's belief in itself; that is, the conviction that we can no longer understand science as one form of possible knowledge, but rather must identify knowledge with science'. All other forms of knowledge, including practitioner knowledge, are considered to be inferior or mistaken versions. What this also suggests is that it is possible to identify a correct method for data collection and if this method is properly applied, then this will inevitably lead to the construction of objective, value-free and authoritative knowledge. However, this generic form of disciplinary knowledge may be rooted in different foundational principles, so that notions of truth, objectivity and authority are understood in different ways. What is shared is a belief in epistemological foundations, and the possibility of the academy producing truthful knowledge, in contradistinction to practical, folkloric or other types of knowledge.

This methodological version of disciplinary knowledge is policed in part by the imposition of a set of procedural values at the stages of examination and validation, where the student is required to meet certain criteria that are broadly accepted by most members of the academic community. They act as a bulwark against the dissolution of academic credibility, but their application acts to include and therefore validate certain types of knowledge and exclude and therefore pathologize other types of knowledge. A tutor on an EngD course reaffirms the importance of this policing role:

Of course, our chief job in my mind is to make sure that we maintain academic quality. I don't want our students to slip into industrial ways of doing things where they tend to try and solve all the problems themselves without referring to literature, where they don't do things systematically and rigorously and thoroughly which is the way things are done in industry. I've worked in industry for most of my life and I know this. Our job is to ensure that they always document things, they always refer back to the proper source, and they think through the logical steps; and that the academic rigour is there and this is what is missing from a lot of industry, in my experience. Industrial practitioners may have doctorates but they slip into the rather slack ways of industrial doing things that, 'yes, well, we know it's this way, we can assume it', and later on they realise that they've got a tower without foundations. It doesn't work properly.

and:

> The academic rigour is still there. I would define academic rigour as basically doing things correctly, making sure everything's done and planned, making sure that you don't get poor analysis – get to change things. Change and then you measure the results.

Underpinning this view is a belief that disciplinary knowledge is superior to knowledge produced in the workplace.

Professional doctorate knowledge may be focussed on practice; but it does not seek to change it in any immediate sense. The student takes on the role of the outsider even if it is research about their own practice or an example of practice that has some resonance with their own. Academic criteria are applied to it, as is exemplified by the co-ordinator of an EdD programme:

> It's a fairly traditional doctoral programme with a very clear focus on research rather than on practice. We're using professional contexts as research sites enabling the student to conduct good quality research.

In this model the theorist and the practitioner are engaged in different activities. Walsh (1993) for instance, suggests that there are four mutually supporting but distinctive kinds of discourses: deliberation, evaluation, science and utopianism. Discourse, he defines, as a mode of enquiry that is logically distinct in some way. The practical setting, in Walsh's third type of discourse, therefore acts as the testing bed for theoretical propositions developed elsewhere, and the student undertaking professional doctorate study is initiated into a practice which is distinct from their workplace practice.

Mode 2: Technical rationality

Whereas Mode 1 knowledge is characterized by an indifference to the practice setting, and the designation of the practice setting as merely the source for theoretical deliberation, Mode 2 knowledge is characterized by a form of technical rationality. Practitioners are required to set to one side their own considered and experience-based ways of conducting themselves at work because these are partial, incomplete and subjective; by contrast they incorporate into their practice scientific knowledge that transcends the local and the particular. Practitioner knowledge is therefore considered to be inferior and incomplete because it is context-dependent, problem-solving, contingent, non-generalizable and is judged not by objective criteria but by whether it contributes to the achievement of short-term goals and problems encountered *in situ*. An assumption is made that the objective knowledge that is produced about programmes, activities and institutions binds the practitioner in particular ways; those ways being the following of rules which can be deduced from that knowledge. Knowledge produced by outsiders, or practitioners behaving as outsiders, is superior to the knowledge produced by practitioners working *in situ*.

The implications for practitioners undertaking academic study is that they should divest themselves of their prior incorrect and incomplete knowledge and adopt precepts based on the objective study of practical activities. Usher *et al.* (1997) describe the role of the practitioner in this mode as a technical and problem-solving activity. It is a view that is concerned with determining a measure of technical efficiency that will necessarily lead to the achievement of predetermined ends and these are separate from the determination of means per se. Lyotard (1984) has argued that knowledge is now constructed and legitimated in terms of its capacity to enhance the efficiency and effectiveness of the economic and social system. He is suggesting that disciplinary modes of knowledge rooted in epistemological foundations no longer have credibility in society, and have been replaced, in the current conditions of postmodernity, by knowledge as the optimizing of efficient performance. Mode 2 knowledge, which may be resisted by academics working with disciplinary forms of knowledge, has become a characteristic of some professional doctorates.

Knowledge in this mode is applied to the practice setting, and indeed its rationale is whether it makes the workplace a more efficient and a more productive place. Mode 2 knowledge may relate to the skill-development of the individual, that is presentational skills; or to the strategic knowledge of the individual in order for him or her to function effectively in the workplace; or to the technical ability of the student so that they can better provide the workplace with solutions to problems that they and others encounter. There is no desire here to examine the various contexts of the work, whether they are political, ethical or consequential. The main criterion for the successful development of this process is whether it works in practice. A tutor on an EngD course reiterates the importance of the technical rationality mode:

> I think by the end of the programme here, the sort of submission of the thesis, I'd be looking for the candidates to be showing clear evidence of being capable of managing research in a commercial organisation and understanding the context, and putting forward good reasons for following particular lines on the research, to make sure that they're not just pursuing an item of knowledge *for its own sake*.

Furthermore, technicist knowledge is buttressed by a notion of evidence-based practice. The practitioner follows the precepts developed by outside researchers, as this EngD co-ordinator suggests:

> But I think the key thing is we're not producing researchers. We're producing people who are end-users of research in their jobs, and in order to be informed end-users, then clearly they need to know about

research in a rather more systematic and structured way than they would if they didn't do a course like this. And I think there's almost a sort of prior point, a sort of more fundamental one which links with the sort of evidence based thing, and the notion that professional practice should be informed by research based knowledge. I mean it is informed by other things as well, but research based knowledge is a prime strand in what should inform professional practice.

EngD's research engineers or students are tutored by both an academic and an industrial mentor. Here an academic tutor on the programme suggests that the divide between academic and professional knowledge is not as wide as it would seem, and that the development of performative knowledge is the end-point for both. Input from the university produces a better product:

> This programme works on several levels. The main team is the research engineer, the academic mentor and the industrial mentor, and again one of the things we found with the EngD is that because of the scope, and some would say the differing requirements of academia and industry; personally, I don't see that myself, I think the two are very complementary. It's difficult to differentiate. Very often there is a difference where the industry wants the answer quickly so they don't do things as rigorously as they have been asked to. But generally, what most people say is that the improvement they get, whether that's made in the loop, reduction in price, improvement in performance or whatever, is generally about half as much again what they would expect they would have got if they simply were doing it as a part of their day to day work. And that's quite a consistent figure, isn't it?

The student learns certain skills, and acquires specific attributes on the programmes of study that enable him or her to perform better in the practice. This mode of knowledge can be contrasted with dispositional knowledge that has affinities with older university agendas.

Mode 3: Dispositional and transdisciplinary knowledge

A different view of the process comprises a belief that it is possible to identify a number of dispositions, liberal in orientation, which through appropriate pedagogic means are taught to students, and the student is better able to go on in the practice as a result of applying them. No end-point is specified so that what works or what behaviours produce the best results are not considered to be relevant criteria for the justification of these forms of knowledge in the guise of dispositional behaviours. The end-point or outcomes of the application of these dispositions is considered to be uncertain, as the dispositions are justified as ends in themselves. A further justification is provided for not designating specific outcomes in the professional workplace and this is that purposes, organizational arrangements and the like cannot be identified outside of the workplace itself and in terms of prevailing conditions. In short, change is such an endemic aspect of workplace life that to specify ends from teaching programmes would render them very quickly out of date. Furthermore, knowledge itself is understood as non-predictable, non-deterministic, situation-specific and contextualized.

One version of this mode of knowledge suggests a non-prescriptive view of the relationship between disciplinary and practice-based knowledges. Texts, both written and oral, produced outside the workplace are understood as useful resources for practitioners, but cannot provide technical knowledge about how to go on in the practice. The various forms of practice impose their own rules on the student-practitioner, and knowledge is constructed in different ways. Methodological imperialism is resisted so that a multi-perspectival view is adopted. There is no one correct method, only a series of methods which groups of researchers and practitioners have developed and which have greater or lesser credence depending on the way those groups are constructed and the influence they have in society. The texts that they produce are stories about the world, which in the process of their telling and re-telling, re-stock or re-story the world itself. They have credence because enough practitioners see them as a useful resource for the solving of practical problems they encounter in their everyday working lives.

Whether or not the practitioner works to the prescriptive framework of the researcher, and implicit within any research text is a set of prescriptions about how the practitioner should behave, will depend on the fit between the values and frameworks held respectively by theorist and practitioner. The outside theorist produces broadly accurate knowledge of educational settings, but the practitioner then adapts and amends it in the light of the contingencies of their own work practices. The practice setting is understood as both the source of and the arena for theoretical development. This viewpoint takes another step away from the technicist position described above.

A more extreme version of Mode 3 knowledge suggests that there may not be a role at all for outside theorists, because they operate outside practice. This perspective construes practice as deliberative action concerned with the making of appropriate decisions about practical problems *in situ*. However, we should not conclude from this that there is no role for theory at all. What is being reconceptualized is the idea of theory itself. Proponents of this view reject the notion of means-end implicit in the technical-rational model and argue that practitioner knowledge does not comprise the making of appropriate technical decisions about applying precepts developed by others. Practitioner knowledge is not just about the identification and application of pre-defined ends, it is also about the designation of ends in the light of deliberative activity about practice. As Usher *et al.* (1997: 127) suggest, practice situations are 'characterised by a complexity and uncertainty which resist routinization'. Such knowledge is and can never be propositional, but always involves continuous cycles of deliberation and action that cannot be transformed in the process into generalizable accounts of educational activities. This closely ties together theory and practice; informal theory central to practice is, as Usher *et al.* (1997) suggest, 'situated theory both entering into and emerging from practice'.

The role of the university, especially with regards to professional doctorates, is to enable practitioners to develop dispositions that enable them to reflect on their own practical experience and go beyond it. A DBA tutor describes the rationale for teaching the first of the compulsory courses students are required to take on her programme:

> Well it's important at a whole range of levels. I mean the DBA itself is very much geared at reflective practice if you like. At the teaching level, again we feel it is important that they build on their experience and bring it in to the classroom, and share that experience with us, as a lot of the learning does. They are supposed to build on the learning outcomes, the learning outcomes are couched around reflection on and development of practical experience. I think that the development of their confidence with theory, in order to use it or structure thinking, is important for them. And later on, I think, they do see it as something important. It is very much based on being able to critique their own work, and that of others. So in a sense I come in to it very practically, and say 'OK we're going to get some ideas'. And one of the first things I suggest they do is critique, using their MBA thesis, or the work of others that they've found, using structures and frameworks for their overall thing. That's how I introduce that topic to them, that they are moving on from their Masters. It's not like more marketing, or more finance, it's a higher level of thinking. It's critique of our knowledges produced, it is different debates in the academic practitioner arena and so on. So I always ask them to draw on their own work, on their own research, whether that be a management report or a critique of their own work, critique the work of others, draw on practical experiences and interactive activities.

Unlike Mode 4 knowledge (see below) where the emphasis is on structural and institutional reform, this form of knowledge is concerned with the development of the individual through reflection. It is about what Freire (1972: 67) describes as reflection upon action: 'a conscious objectification of their own and others' actions through investigation, contemplation and comment'.

The reflection occurs in relation to the activity under examination and is therefore action-based. The student sees their practice in a different light, which means that the decisions they make in relation to future actions are different. Schon (1987) characterizes it as a continuous interrogation and imaginative reconstruction of the practitioner's actions as they are unfolding. A DBA tutor describes the process in the following way:

> My sense of it is [that] it is very professionally related to them and they do see it as a vehicle for career progression. For those who are already at

the top of their career, or as high as they want to go, very often it is sort of providing them with the space to reflect on their practice and to think of new strategies or new understandings of what they're doing.

Another form of self-reflection is specifically epistemological in character and involves a re-evaluation of their knowledge perspectives. This comprises examination of prevailing assumptions about knowledge, and a discarding of those assumptions with the possibility of replacing them at a later stage. In that those ideas give the student a sense of security, this may lead to a deep sense of insecurity and confusion. The purpose of the pedagogical activity on some professional doctorate courses is to dissolve, fragment or otherwise disrupt the models of knowledge held by students. There is no attempt made to provide a replacement, since the purpose is to provide disjuncture in the minds of students, and the responsibility for replacement is devolved to the student. An EdD tutor exemplifies this point:

> The main purpose of that weekend is to get them to start thinking critically about what is research and to begin to think themselves as developing an identity as a researcher. And, as is so often the case, they come along with very specific ideas about what is legitimate, valid research, very often fairly traditional notions about that which is sometimes partly a product of their background. I don't know how many in terms of numbers but we tend to have a fair amount of people with psychological degrees, first degrees in Psychology. They'll often be people who have very positive and negative views on what constitutes research so a major aim of the first weekend is to get them to begin to question their assumptions about that fixed position. One of the things that I've put a lot of store on, this is to do with me and where I'm coming from, it's to do with a life historical approach, because a lot of my work is to do with life history, that's my specialism if you like. So we do have a life history workshop which looks at their education and their research career to date, and looks at where they have got these ideas from, what's it to do with, what's happened to them and how might that colour their views and perceptions about research. I get them to think about how it is that they ended up being here in the first instance, on this particular degree programme, and what are the things that have contributed to that. So, that's something that I see as being quite significant and important. They might end up coming right back to where they'd started but at least they know that they're more informed of the context of that particular thing and also they are more kind of technically and critically positioned by the time that they do so. My experience is that, by and large, even if they go back and want to do that sort of research for themselves, they're aware and they're more open-minded than they were.

Furthermore, within this programme, there is an attempt made to relate their present orientation to their past experiences, in particular to their own educational experiences:

I think something else that we do during that first weekend, I think we probably do quite successfully, David does a session on the history of education, which links the things which have happened and the methodologies that have been important at particular times with political concerns and economic concerns; and then, by doing the life history thing and thinking about their own education, in the context of what's happened to them, what sorts of schools did they go to, did they go to grammar schools, secondary moderns, it begins to become much more pertinent to them as people and perhaps that helps them to begin to make that move away from thinking 'oh well, you know, we've got to be objective, we've got to be positivist', because actually at the end of the day, this is people's lives we're talking about. Educational research affects people's lives. It affects my life, it affects my kids' lives and so on and so forth, and, I think by doing that, by linking in educational research and research generally with political and global thinking more generally, that does perhaps make it a bit easier for them to say, 'well, that's one way of doing it, perhaps there are other considerations that I ought to bear in mind'. We do plug away a bit about this question of assumptions and being critical and emphasizing that. And then of course we point them in the direction and supply them with a wide range of different readings to make them aware, and it's not uncommon by the end of the first full day for people to say, 'You know I never thought about that, it's such a new notion'.

Gibbons *et al.*'s (1994: 27) Mode 2 knowledge has some affinities with this form of knowledge, in that it is trans-disciplinary, judged by whether it works or not, pragmatic in orientation, situated within the workplace, has loose quality control, and derives its context from the work itself: 'Working in an application context creates pressures to draw upon a diverse array of knowledge resources and to configure them according to the problem in hand'. However, the university has a role in the process in so far as the practitioner is required to go beyond their current ways of thinking and behaving. In order to do this, the student develops appropriate dispositions and acquires the requisite amount of reflective capital to transform their own practice and ways of working. This mode of knowledge is essentially concerned with the individual and their own practice. It is therefore limited in scope. Mode 4 knowledge has wider purposes.

Mode 4: Critical knowledge

Here the purpose is explicitly or implicitly political and change-orientated. Knowledge is understood as critical, that is critical of the prevailing ethos and purposes of the various workplaces. As one EdD student puts it: 'a kind of critical reflection on things that people would prefer not to have critical reflection applied to'. Individuals are positioned within discursive and institutional structures that influence how they understand themselves and others and how they can change both themselves and the institutions in which they work. The professional doctorate therefore has as one of its purposes interventions in the field and the imposition of a set of values on the workings of the organization, how it functions, what it produces and what are its effects. Its concerns are fundamentally to do with identifying power structures in society and destabilizing these, to the end that more equal and more just arrangements are made. An EdD co-ordinator here reflects on the work of one of their students:

> I can give you one example of that. This is a student down in Somerset, working within his school, looking at value addedness and target setting and so on. The school itself established this programme of target setting and value added approaches and so on. The student has been doing this degree for three years and has been developing a critical appraisal, if you like, of some of these processes. He's now coming up against the fact that the head teacher does not want him to circulate, disseminate this information. In other words, he's not behaving as a practitioner; he's more concerned to develop the programmes in a theoretical sense. He's concerned about issues to do with whether the information they're collecting is actually valid and reliable. So there are tensions that he has to resolve. I mean, you could argue, I suppose, that a good programme in a school should take account of these things. But it's not actually the way the practitioners understand the developmental programme within their school – tensions that he has to resolve. I think it's to do with the nature of knowledge as well. Academics have a much sharper sense and are likely to reject as unsound knowledge that can be used practically. So, for example, this particular student, is arguing that this is 'unsound knowledge', whereas the head teacher is saying, 'No, it's not. It works. It's good enough for us'. So there are different criteria being applied. They're applying different criteria as to what counts as valid knowledge within the institution in which the student is working. And I think that's one of the tensions between practitioner and academic knowledge.

This account by an EdD co-ordinator also focuses on how knowledge of this type can disrupt current and conventional power arrangements:

> There's another question which is to do with power, and you may work in an absolutely intolerable, unbearable place, where relations of power are very oppressive and not necessarily be aware of it. Then you start doing some research and, through the process of finding out about what you're doing, you start to see things that you didn't see before. Now that's, I think, quite a deep issue in practice settings, and also with this kind of doctorate, there is a sense in which in practice, in the schools or colleges or whatever, there are certain things that it is important that they remain tacit. And clearly what the EdD student perhaps is doing is making them explicit. And when you first become aware of

something like that, is not a time when you're very good at keeping quiet about it. If you've been doing research for a long time, you can go into a school, you can be very quiet, you can be very careful, and you can conduct it in such a way that you will not bring up lots of resistance. But when you've just discovered it and you're in the middle of it, you must be burning, aren't you? The power dynamics of being, a sort of dual multiple identities and having this identity of a researcher and a sort of an affiliation with the university and a practitioner or a worker, and how you manage these different sort of identities and roles and responsibilities is complex. And they're two different things. A fourth point as well, I think the difference is, again taking the example of the student in Somerset, schools tend to take on board what governments tell them to do. They tend to treat government documents, even government research reports in a very uncritical manner. And along comes my student and says, 'No, this is not the way you should be reading these documents. You should be reading them in a critical way.' And this is an anathema to many people who are working as practitioners.

This student is seeking to problematize a specific aspect of their practice, not with the intention of finding a technical solution but to understand what is happening, and this redescription is in opposition to current political discourses. This fourth mode of knowledge may be contrasted with disciplinarity, technical rationality and dispositionality in that it attempts to undermine conventional knowledge discourses within which most practitioners work and in the process undermine the legitimacy of institutional life.

Hybridity

Disciplinarity is characterized by an indifference to the practice setting, the practice setting is understood as the source for reflection, but not the arena in which that theorizing takes place. Students are initiated into academic practices that have their own set of rules, and their task is to imbibe the culture of the new setting into which they are being initiated. Technical rationality, on the other hand, is characterized by a view of knowledge that prioritizes outsider knowledge over practice-based knowledge, and the practitioner acts in a technicist manner. Dispositionality identifies certain virtues, an example of which is a capacity to engage in various forms of meta-reflection about practice and identity that enable the practitioner to go on in the practice and embrace change. The fourth of our modes of knowledge is criticality, and here the student-practitioner develops the capacity to reflect critically on the discourses, mores and ways of working of the institution of which they are a member, with the intention of changing it.

What happens in practice is that these modes of knowledge are compromised in various ways. These integrating tendencies may take a number of forms. The first is adaptation, where the different knowledge modes are represented in the aims of the programme and an attempt is made to meet all their requirements, even if at different times on the programme. Thus a programme may operate through disciplinary, technicist, dispositional and critical modes of knowledge. This is only possible where the different practices have evolved so that the tensions between the different modes of knowledge have been partly or fully resolved and therefore do not threaten the coherence of the partnership activities. For example, a discipline may have evolved so that relations with the practice setting are implicit within its rules of operation. Or critical or dispositional modes of knowledge are gradually re-defined so that either they are an implicit part of the practice setting and thus do not act to threaten its integrity in any way, or built into the practice setting is a set of mechanisms which allow it unproblematically to absorb knowledge which is critical of previous practice-based knowledge. One of the consequences of this is that weak boundaries are established between the academy and the practice setting. The EngD more closely aligns itself with this model.

On the other hand, there are forms of integration which are more problematic, and where tensions are present between these different modes of knowledge. One such form is colonization where a mode of knowledge is so powerful that it effectively subsumes other modes of knowledge. Here, the student undertaking professional doctorate study is required to put to one side their ways of working and assume those that characterize another mode of knowledge. Disciplinary practices sometimes act in this way so that the student is required to conform to the rules that underpin it, regardless of their current orientation. The academy acts to colonize the practice setting and impose its ways of working on the workplace. Here strong boundaries are maintained between the different practices. The EdD and the DBA at times displayed these colonizing tendencies.

A third form of integration is where the practice setting becomes the dominant partner in the relationship and is not only understood as the source for theoretical development but as the arena in which this activity takes place. The role of the university is confined to the development of appropriate dispositions, but even here identification of those dispositions is understood in terms of relevance to the practice setting. Universities are therefore as players in the game required to move much more into the territory of the practice setting and adjust their way of working so that knowledge is produced which has practical applications, whether that knowledge is dispositional or technical in character. Here, a form of colonization takes place but works in the opposite direction to the form expressed above.

The student, as a result, has to negotiate between communities of practice, and within the various hybrid forms they may take. The student is required to be a part of their practice setting and be conversant with the language, behaviour registers, and specific repertoires of meaning of that setting. Participants form close relationships and develop idiosyncratic ways of engaging with one another that outsiders cannot easily enter. They have a detailed and complex understanding of their enterprise as they define it, which outsiders may not share. They have developed a repertoire for which outsiders miss shared references (Wenger 1998). At the same time, they are required to gain entry to another setting, that of the discipline in which they are now working. As we have already suggested, the framework within which they have to perform may be adapted or colonized in various ways. What this means is that gaining entry to both academic and practice settings takes on a different form and structure.

Furthermore, entry to these sites of knowledge is rarely an easy process, and full acceptance is achieved in stages. The disciplinary setting opens itself up to allow entry by modifying its entry requirements so that the student is allowed peripheral participation in that community (Lave and Wenger 1991). Peripherality provides an approximation to full participation, so that the student instead of being exposed to the full repertoire of meanings immediately is offered in the first instance an approximation of them. This leads in turn to access to the full repertoire.

There are two possible processes at work. First, one repertoire may seek to become the dominant mode in the mind of the student and there is little negotiation of that repertoire. Here strong boundaries are maintained between the two communities of practice. Or the boundaries are weak and both communities of practice are subject to change and modification as a result of the interchange; and change happens as a result of negotiating meanings and practices. This is a two-staged process: at the level of peripherality and at the level of full membership.

These four modes of knowledge: disciplinarity, technical rationality, dispositionality and criticality are ideal and operate in different ways in professional doctorate programmes. Programmes may be constructed as disciplinary forms of knowledge, but rapidly assume, not least in the minds of students, a critical form. Furthermore, at different points and in different places programmes operate through different modes of knowledge. In each arena and at different times, different modes of knowledge-construction may take precedence. Gibbons *et al.*'s (1994) distinction between Mode 1 and Mode 2 knowledge provides some purchase on the types of hybrid knowledges produced on professional doctorates, but restricts understanding by contrasting the one against the other. This chapter has suggested a fourfold model to shed light on the construction of knowledge within professional doctorate programmes. The next chapter examines in greater detail the process of importation of ideas, especially in so far as it relates to the relationship between different sites of knowledge construction.

5

The Reflective Student-Practitioner

Introduction

In the last chapter, we identified a possible tension between the two sites of practice within which the professional doctorate student is expected to work. A range of relationships is being established between the academy and the workplace, and these reflect institutional and disciplinary histories and different understandings of the theory-practice relation. Here an EdD student reflects on his experience of study, and identifies a way in which his practice has changed:

> I've also tried to link what I do at work with what I do on the EdD. What I've written on the EdD goes on a file and then at work something will come up or there will be another briefing on a policy document, and quite often I can go to the file and pull out work that I've already done for the EdD. I've already done a lot of the homework and the background reading to produce a policy paper that they're asking for. I've been talking to some other students a few weeks ago and one of them was sort of saying that it was a bit of a schizophrenic experience. You had your hat on as a student and a hat as a professional practitioner, but then it was a comfortable schizophrenia in that everybody was saying it was a space in which to look at and reflect on the way in which you operated as a professional practitioner and almost a different lens to look through how you functioned on a day-to-day basis. I think if anything I've become more of a student in my professional practice, so I've become that sort of reflective practitioner through the EdD.

Reflection and reflective practices have become central ideas for the construction of professional development courses in a range of disciplines. Schon's (1987) well-known distinction between reflection-in-action and reflection on reflection-in-action is a useful starting point for our discussion of the processes students go through in their attempts to mediate between the two communities of practice within which they are located. Argyris and

Schon (1978) make a further distinction between theories-in-use and espoused theories, where the former refers to the type of reflection which goes on within the daily activity of the practitioner and which results in theories-in-action, and espoused theory which involves reflection and is the way we express those theories-in-action to other people. The articulation and theorization of reflection-in-action therefore involves a going beyond and reformulation of the original process of reflection.

They make a further distinction between single-loop and double-loop learning, where the former is described as limited to reflection about the loop between the action strategy and that which results from it, while the latter in addition involves reflection on the underlying purposes, frameworks and values with which the organization is concerned, what Argyris and Schon call 'governing variables':

> When the error detected and corrected permits the organisation to carry on its present policies or achieve its present objectives, then that error-and-correction process is *single-loop* learning. Single-loop learning is like a thermostat that learns when it is too hot or too cold and turns the heat on or off. The thermostat can perform this task because it can receive information (the temperature of the room) and take corrective action. *Double-loop* learning occurs when error is detected and corrected in ways that involve the modification of an organisation's underlying norms, policies and objectives.
>
> (1978: 2–3)

These distinctions are useful, and will be expanded upon in the development of a model to explain professional doctorate activity. Reflective activity may be proximal to or distanced from the object of reflection, and this is best illustrated by the difference between reflection-in-action and reflection on reflection-in-action. This last can take a number of forms and more importantly directions. The direction for the reflective process can be from practice to articulation to meta-theorizing about that reflection or about the activity or about the consequences of that activity; or it can take a different direction so that the original spur for the subsequent reflection comes from outside the workplace setting and is then imported into it, subsequently influencing it. Furthermore, the direction for the reflection may not take a linear form, but comprises a complicated synthesis between the three types of reflection identified so far: reflection-in-action, reflection about reflection-in-action, and meta-reflection about the activity and subsequent reflection which now inheres in it.

As we have suggested, one of the principal aims of professional doctorate courses is the development of the reflective practitioner. This is understood in a variety of ways. In the first case, the emphasis is on the practitioner with an assumption being made that if the student both learns how to be more reflective and is allowed to operate in conditions that enable these skills to be put into practice, then the practice of the student will be improved. In the second case, the emphasis is on reflection with again an implicit assumption being made that reflection is a virtue in its own right. This process may cause the student to know more about their practice, but the purpose is not change or improvement to that practice, but deeper and more profound understandings of the practice setting in which the student works. Indeed, it is feasible to suggest that deeper understandings of the practice setting may lead to the student becoming a less effective practitioner. It is possible to imagine a situation in which reflection either causes the practitioner to surface and therefore become more self-conscious about the setting which results in less spontaneous actions and behaviours and therefore less effective practice; or that wider and deeper understandings of what the practitioner is doing in the workplace may lead him or her to question the moral basis of their actions so that they are less likely to be able to perform effectively.

The key to understanding this conundrum is the different purposes of the reflective activity and in turn the different relationships that this reflection may have to action. Within the three doctorate programmes, a number of different reflective strategies were being employed by students for coursework or thesis writing. These were: reflection-in-action; reflection on reflection in action; reflection on reflection-in-action which then leads to planned change to practice; reflection-in-action as the re-naming and re-framing of professional practice; reflection-in-action as problem solving; intrinsic reflexive awareness in relation to identity; and extrinsic reflexive awareness in relation to action and situational constraint.

This chapter will examine these various forms of reflection, integral to learning, and the way some of these types of learning are prioritized or marginalized as students undertake professional doctorate study. Reflective practices have become central to professional development courses in the last few years, especially as courses are constructed with the aim of integrating practitioner experience, workplace learning and academic study. Incorporating these reflective practices into the repertoires of students has occasioned some criticisms. These focus on the affective dimension of learning so that students are not encouraged to explore 'inner discomforts' (Brookfield 1987); the technicist nature of the reflective activity undertaken (Boud and Walker 1998); the unreflexive and decontextualized form of this reflective behaviour (Usher *et al.* 1997); the lack of criticality implicit in the reflective activity; and the uncritical acceptance of experience as the driver for change within the workplace (Boud and Walker 1998). In the last chapter we suggested that practitioners undertaking professional doctorate study are positioned within particular knowledge frames and that this influences their work on the doctorate programmes and how this relates to and influences their workplace practices. Here we will develop a number of different models of reflection-in-learning as they relate to professional doctorate study.

Focus of reflection

Reflection by the student-practitioner is focussed on one or more aspect of the piece. In the course of the study-programme, attention may switch between areas of interest; and the written product may refer to a range of foci with an attempt made to make connections between them. These foci are: the practitioners' activity within the workplace setting; self-identity and the practitioner's life course; policy in relation to the workplace setting; organizational structures within the practitioner's workplace; and the innovation or external change object.

Workplace focus

The first of these is the activities usually performed by the student-practitioner in their workplace. The engineering doctorate is structured as placement-learning so that the student in the initial phases may be an out-sider or only have peripheral membership of the workplace (Lave and Wenger 1991). Professional doctorate students on the DBA and the EdD are located within a specific workplace to which they make reference and indeed on which they focus their research. Thus within the three professional doc-torates, there may be a range of relationships to the workplace setting and therefore a range of specifiable workplace activities on which the student can focus their attention. Typically a student works as a research engineer or alongside other research engineers (as in the EngD); or as a senior manager within a school or college (as in the EdD); or as a business manager (as in the DBA). They will have different degrees of knowledge about their practice, much of which will be tacit, but fairly easily surfaced by the practitioner if they so wish. These can take a procedural, technical or relational form.

Wenger (1998) describes these procedural rules or characteristics of a community of practice in the following way. Members of that community have established dependency relationships with other members of the com-munity and as a result have developed a shared way of going on in the practice. The practice itself is characterized by rapid flows of information; the absence of introductory preambles and an implied knowledge of what other members know. When a problem occurs, its content is understood in terms of an agreed framework, and discussion of this framework is implicit. Identifying moments and orientations are shared and negotiated within the group itself. Specific forms of communication including specialist registers and vocabularies are adopted which are not transparent to the outsider; and the member is located within a shared discourse or way of looking at the world.

Technical knowledge, on the other hand, is defined as those skills, attrib-utes and know-how which allow the practitioner to work with the organ-izational product. Shulman (1987) provides an example in relation to teachers and lecturers when he suggests that there are seven broad areas of knowledge with which they need to be acquainted: content knowledge; general pedagogical knowledge, with special reference to those broad principles and strategies of management and organization that appear to transcend the subject matter; curriculum knowledge with particular grasp of the materials and programmes that serve as 'tools of the trade' for teachers; pedagogical content knowledge, that special amalgam of content and pedagogy that is uniquely the province of teachers, their own special form of professional understanding; knowledge of learners and their characteristics; knowledge of educational contexts, ranging from the workings of the group to the character of communities and cultures; and knowledge of educational ends, purposes and values, and their philosophical and historical grounds. Research engineers and business management students would in turn need to acquire specialist technical knowledge in order to function in the workplace.

The third type of practical knowledge is relational. A workplace practice is constructed by internal and external relations. Procedural rules regulate internal relations, however, externality occasions a second set of rules. These refer to the relations between similar institutional units; the relations between institutions and regulating bodies such as governments and government agencies; and the relations between the institutional product and the market in which it is ultimately placed. These relations are corrective, directive or advisory. However, the flow of power is rarely one way but operates at different points and in different directions.

A focus on identity

The second possible focus for reflection is self-identity and the practitioner's life-course. Chapters 8 and 9 offer illustrations of the way reflection on identity is integral to the completion of a professional doctorate. For example, intrinsic reflexive awareness understands that person as more than just a practitioner who performs certain activities at work and usually in the workplace. This type of reflection stretches the person through time and relates to the life-course of the individual. An example is provided here by an EdD student:

> And then I had a meeting with my tutor, and she said: 'what really does interest you?' I was trying to think of something that really interests me. She said: 'What's coming from the heart', and what I always think back to is my own education and the 11+ and the effect it had on me when I was never entered for the 11+ – the whole issue of selection and self-esteem. And of course the job I've got at school is sort of Head of Lower School, induction of new children. I decided to look at selection and self-esteem and eventually what was decided was some sort of topic to do with coping strategies and failure; but to reverse it, and look at how failure was coped with by middle class rather than working class

children, because they have expectations of passing and don't. So I decided to find a sample of about five or six people in their forties who had actually failed the 11+. And then sort of interview them about their life to see how that initial failure had affected them and what coping strategies they used.

The relationship to his practice is indirect. The reflective activity is focussed on a painful episode in his life, and he has chosen a proxy situation that he hopes will resonate with his earlier experiences. Learning in this case is therefore biographically contextualized. Other types of contextualization are also important. Usher (1997) suggests in relation to finding out about the world that knowledge has a con-text, pre-text, sub-text and inter-text. Learning is a textual practice. The con-text comprises the situatedness of the learner in the act of learning so that they are immersed in structures or significations of gender, sexuality, ethnicity, class, and the like. Furthermore, the learner is situated within various pre-texts or discourses about the way the world is structured so that the learning strategy is underpinned by pre-organized meanings. The pre-text has attached to it a sub-text, in that the learning strategy and the knowledge that is subsumed within it are distinctive ways of knowing the world. Finally, each learning setting makes reference to other forms of learning, other knowledge constructs and other historical meaning formations – the inter-text. The con-text, pre-text, sub-text and inter-text provide the essential base for learning. They are integral to every episode of learning that involves the learner in focusing on an aspect of their practice or an aspect of their self.

A focus on policy

The third area that students focussed on was the policy process, and indeed, some professional doctorates offered students courses on policy and the relationship between policy and practice within their disciplinary matrix. Students' work examined the fragmented, non-linear, contested nature of the policy relay, where original intentions are rarely fulfilled in practice. The focus of their work was therefore on those external relations to the work-place and not on the workplace itself or on workplace products.

A DBA student whose research work focussed on the discrepancy between policy and practice provides an example of this here:

My thesis examined the concept of entrapment, which generally is in the field of new product development. I was examining why people pursue new product development projects in the face of rational economic theory. This issue was a key feature of the way in which the public sector was moving but had not benefited from any evaluation. There was no requirement for my project to be linked to my own professional practice. As an outcome for my thesis I developed a model for avoidance of entrapment which helped me with new forms of product development.

I think that a key result from my work is that people now realise that there needs to be a sound business case in the public sector for major change agendas round product development (particularly in local government). I have discussed this with a number of people in the cabinet office and I feel that there is a growing awareness that entrapment occurs in the public sector as much as in the private, and new technology has all the characteristics of entrapment if allowed to go unchecked.

In identifying discontinuities between policy and practice, an attempt is made to either influence policy or change practice so that it conforms to the policy interdiction. It is also interesting to note that this student was as concerned to change policy as he was to change practice so that it was better aligned with policy.

A focus on the institution

A fourth focus for reflection for students was institutional. We have already suggested that the key to understanding the type of reflection undertaken by students is its focus, and in relation to this, the end-point in the mind of the student as to the reason for doing this reflection in the first place. Schon defines reflection-in-action in the following ways:

> The practitioner allows himself [sic] to experience surprise, puzzlement, or confusion in a situation which he finds uncertain or unique. He reflects on the phenomenon before him, and on the prior understandings which have been implicit in his behaviour. He carries out an experiment which serves to generate both a new understanding of the phenomenon and a change in the situation.
>
> (Schon 1983: 63)

> When a practitioner makes sense of a situation he perceives to be unique, he sees it as something already present in his repertoire. To see *this* site as *that* one is not to subsume the first under a familiar category or rule. It is, rather, to see the unfamiliar, unique situation as both similar to and different with respect to it. The familiar situation functions as a precedent, or a metaphor, or . . . an exemplar for the unfamiliar one.
>
> (Schon 1983: 138)

Taking Schon's theories as a whole, there are some significant weaknesses. The most important of these is the inability of the theory to sustain a notion of triple-loop learning, in that the practitioner, far from being isolated within the workplace, is in fact influenced by external forces. This is especially pertinent in the case of the student-practitioner who is required to import ideas into their own practice. Single-loop reflection-in-action then, is a process in which the practitioner identifies a problem, frames a possible solution, tests out that solution, evaluates the success or otherwise of that solution and embeds this new practice into their repertoire, so that it becomes a routine part of their day-to-day activity. It is only revisited if it occasions a new problem; however, the identification of the problem and the identification of the solution always takes place within tacit and therefore unexamined assumptions held by the practitioner about the organizational structures, power relations, purposes and values of the workplace setting itself. This process of knowledge construction is situation-specific, cannot be applied to other settings, expands the repertoire of action knowledge of the practitioner, and is oral, impermanent and not formally codified.

Double-loop reflection-in-action involves a further process of reflection in that the practitioner explicitly directs their attention to wider concerns so that the problem and the solution are framed by organizational structures and indeed may extend to political and social structures external to the organization itself. As we have already suggested, the direction is non-linear and not even uni-directional but may involve visiting and revisiting the various parts of the model until a solution is found. Clearly the action part of the reflection has wider implications beyond the immediate workplace practices of the practitioner.

A further stage is what Schon calls reflection on reflection-in-action. Here reflective work is performed on work already undertaken so that a meta-process is set in motion. The focus is still on the activities of the practitioner, but now the emphasis shifts to the reflective activity that was an implicit part of the reflection-in-action. Again, this process may occasion a third type of learning, which has been called triple-loop learning. As with double-loop learning we are not suggesting a linear form, and indeed because of its further complexity, the influence is multi-directional and each site is implicated to different degrees at different moments. The focus of activity may be at the level of immediate practice, institutional or extra-institutional; and depending on which level will occasion or lead to different types of action. Further to this, the level on which the practitioner is focusing will determine how the problem is treated, and whether a process of re-naming and re-framing is set in motion. Indeed, the problem may within this process no longer come to be conceptualized as a problem and therefore requires no solution, though this meta-process may provide the practitioner with a different type of problem requiring correspondingly a different type of solution. In short, this adds to the complexity of the model being proposed here because reflection on reflection-in-action may lead to either an unreflexive process of change (the production of technicist knowledge); or to a critical perspective and thus radical change (depending on circumstances and thus leading to the development of critical forms of knowledge); or to a detached form of understanding which has no immediate relationship to action (and has direct affinities with disciplinary forms of knowledge).

We have identified a range of foci and suggested that drawing a distinction between reflection-in-action and reflection on reflection-in-action, as Schon does, misleadingly simplifies what is in fact a much more complicated set of processes. Here, an EdD student describes how he developed different models for determining value-addedness within his institution. His reflective activity comprises in part processes of abstraction and generalization by making reference to other settings and other systems:

> One of the things that I do at my school is value-added as part of the YELIS and ALIS projects at the University of Durham. YELIS is the Year Eleven Indicator System and ALIS is the Advanced Level Indicator System. And I was involved in setting it up in the school in 1994 and 1995 and I'd been very keen on the idea of looking at how you can measure how effective teaching is. And I suppose another incentive that came along was the idea of performance management, threshold assessment, and so I was quite interested in that. And I suppose because I have a personal hat on this, as it were, in my school, I was thinking can you measure teachers by a single statistic. And clearly with the new Labour government the writing was on the wall, using the value-added measure, the pupil progress measure. It was a case study in the school where I worked, and it was very much collecting interview data; looking at documentary material. I'm talking about original sorts of meetings, reports written internally, comments made by staff on various question- naires. So it was really extracting information. The other side was the quantitative part. It was very much number-crunching, value added data. What I did was disaggregate the data and looked at it in terms of individual teachers. It was very much in my school and was live in the sense that it was linked to performance management which is obviously very new now, and threshold assessment. You see one of the things I was heavily involved in was the training aspect – telling staff how to fill in threshold forms; and it was quite interesting that staff might come up to me and say: 'I don't think I'm going to apply for the threshold assess- ment'. And I say: 'why'. And they'd say 'Well I had a sort of Maths set 4 and they got a value added of minus 0.6 so that means I'm not a good teacher'. You know a lot of people were very demoralised. And I would say to them: 'My research says that it doesn't show that'. And I was able to encourage people. But the number at the end of the day, I suppose, that is what the research concluded, the number is not telling you everything about the teacher.

The student-practitioner here has imported into his workplace a model for determining value-addedness and he has then evaluated whether it works or not in his specific workplace. However, his reflections take him beyond the technical effectiveness of the innovation. He is beginning here to question the ethical basis of the innovation itself.

Reflection on practice may involve surfacing intuitive knowledge and reworking existing vocabularies. For this student, the knowledge being con- structed by her has consequences that were not easily foreseen and placed her in a difficult situation:

How do you go out there and carry out a policy that's quite blatantly wrong, but you're told you have to do it. But it makes it very difficult when you deconstruct the notion of special educational needs, and you're going round having to take part in hospital assessments using terminology you feel is oppressive. Most of the time, you learn to forget it and compartmentalise your kind of knowledge. That's what I mean about this whole thing. It's not simple putting together theory and practice. I think that there are loads of people who pretend that it's a nice smooth continuum and it's not, you know. And one thing I'm trying to do is set up a discussion group with my colleagues because I'm in quite a subversive team, and that's what keeps me going, and I'm trying to set up these discussion groups to talk about things like deconstruction. I deal with special educational needs and there has been some interest and it's going to be a real challenge for me to see if I can do this, and in a way quite frightening, because it's like having to politicise people, and that's a very dangerous thing in the workplace.

Triple-loop learning then focuses critically on both the internal dynamics of the workplace, the way the student-practitioner is positioned by intra- and extra- institutional discourses, and those external factors that serve to define the institution itself. However, learning involving importation, and reflection on structural impediments may also be technicist as well as critical.

Importation or a focus on innovation

The key to understanding the more complicated model being proposed here is to examine importation or the way ideas as a result of reflection are imported into the student's repertoire. We have already suggested that the practitioner may be focusing on different aspects of the whole picture, so they could be examining particular aspects of policy or they could be examining the policy process as it impacts on their own or their institution's practice. They could be doing this in a number of different ways depending on the type of knowledge construction that is taking place. Here, an EdD student reflects on his time as a professional doctorate student:

I'm far more questioning, far more penetrating and analytical about all sorts of things. I know how to think round things a lot more than I used to. I'm not so accepting of old morals and traditional modes of working and I have very clear ideas about new ways of working in line with more understanding of psychology and education. Because I suppose that its inevitable that this sort of level of learning and understanding challenges conventions in the system in which we work, and that certainly happened to me. It's very hard, actually, in my role to try to bring what I've learnt into a way, a process which becomes accepted by the people with whom I'm working. And it's a thorny issue because no longer do I sit and think. I actually say 'There's another way of looking at this, have you thought of this', and everyone goes quiet and gives me that look: 'you're not supposed to say that'. You know as a headteacher I was used to writing reports and documents, but this has taken it onto a higher plane, a different set of vocabulary, a different set of jargon. So there are various aspects of research that I'd undertaken that have directly benefited things. Just by looking at something, you change it. Therefore we are looked at as outsiders. So therefore it is very difficult to import knowledge and to actually use it in the system. The system doesn't want to use it. And there are all sorts of reasons why it is actually very hard to change practice with what we gain, and this is a serious issue because organisations have got to move on and we've got to help them to look at things differently. Instead of treating us as almost outsiders, we're inside but we're outside.

He is making a number of points here about the relationship between theory and practice. First, he has now acquired knowledge of generalizable theories of education and psychology, and a new language for describing his practice. Second, he has developed a belief that if he could import these theories into the practices of his staff, this would improve their practice. Third, he accepts that importing this knowledge into the system is difficult, if not impossible. Finally, at the end of the piece, he is beginning to articulate a theory that connects outsider and insider knowledge. In a fundamental sense what he is doing is developing a theory of change that as we saw in the previous chapter has its origins in a technicist mode of knowledge delivered through a powerful insider within the organization. With this model, practitioners re-name and re-frame their practice in the light of theoretical knowledge developed elsewhere, and this re-naming and re-framing inevitably leads to changes in practice for the better. This is one model of change, and our exemplar headteacher here articulates some problems with it.

Another model of importation involves the student in identifying a problem in the practice setting, asking key practitioners for their solutions, evaluating the options presented to him, trying them out in practice, evaluating the results, and finally amending the model:

The subject actually from the academic point of view I was interested in was knowledge transfer, the power of knowledge or rather the process of knowledge transfer, and particularly when coming across complex issues and problems. So my practical subject is globalisation of telecommunications business environments. So I said, 'Well, but how?' I said, 'well, will there be enough material to cover and how will I get access to the materials and organisation'. So I had to narrow it down to my environment, which in my country is the telecommunications business environment. I had to develop my methodology in order to achieve my research objective. I found a methodology called SODA (Strategy Options Development and Analysis). So that took me into managerial cognition aspects. So anyway, I developed my methodology and I made a literature review. So then I selected five organisations, three from the private sector and two ministries from the public sector, and I interviewed the managing director, the general manager and the regulator; and I used the cognitive model, sometimes called cognitive mapping— organising thoughts, patterns and mental models. So I was interested in knowledge, don't forget my aim was interest in knowledge. And while I was developing the methodology I had devised, I was applying the SODA, but it didn't work. So, I had to modify it and I called this ASODA (Adapted, Strategic, Option, Development and Analysis), and from that I devised the VIMO method (Views, Issues, Impact and Options). So I went back to the players and they used it and identified a number of VIMOs. So then I conducted workshops for everyone to build the concept into their mind, and then to make things interesting to them because they could see things are happening and there is benefit for them. That was Phase 2. And then I went to the regulators and the third phase was the players and the regulators in workshops. The research ended with some practical changes within the different organisations because they all knew about all the others' issues and in the way the regulators conducted their business.

What characterizes this approach? A problem is identified, in this case a lack of direction and co-operation between a number of companies in relation to the issue of globalization. The student then attempts to discover what the problem is, and asks participants for possible solutions, all the while suggesting to them a possible model for resolving their disagreements. The purpose of the research is to devise a strategy by which a number of disparate companies can come together and produce an agreed solution to a problem that affects all of them. This methodology is tested and retested, and the final stage is to persuade those companies and the regulators to put it into practice.

A variation on this is where the student develops an organizational strategy from the literature, then tests it out, evaluates its success or otherwise in their workplace, then modifies it in relation to the evaluation, and finally, writes an account of what happened. The development of a programme involves strategic decisions to be made about how it can best be delivered, so the student tests it in a number of situations and then develops a model of the best possible way of delivering it, in other words, identifying institutional barriers and ways of overcoming them. Methods of delivery are tested and then modified in response to this testing.

Importation of theory may be developed outside the workplace, but the model is constructed so that it can be operationalized in the workplace. What this means is that the research engineer needs to understand the culture in which the innovation is going to be implanted. In other words, there are a number of different practical applications of the theory and what is important for the student is that within the current ways of working of the industry the people within it are able to use it to continue to develop the product. This doesn't imply that the workplace into which the innovation is being imported is incapable of change, only that the innovation when it is being applied does not go too far beyond the ways of working and understanding currently in use:

> Because they're a small company, they have no need for people with specifically blue skies research orientations. And the control valve industry is a very black art as well – it's very difficult for research organisations because you need someone that's really working closely with the company all the time to really understand that black art. So the benefits to them is proper academic research that's not been done; and if you look at some of the papers on control value design, they just said: 'Oh, we'll stick it in a test and we'll see what happens'. And they called that academic research, and that's not academic research. It's not a detailed study and it's not a thorough study. And what I have done is just brought the academic in to the commercial environment. So that's the benefit the company has seen. From my point of view, it's meant I've applied that academic research in a commercial organisation which has meant that I've gained a massive amount. I understand both sides of the story which is an obvious advantage. I can talk to other academics or I can talk to the commercial people.

These examples of importation all have built into them notions of testing theory in the workplace. The driver for the student is whether it works in practice. Knowledge, though situationally specific, is still technicist in orientation. The three forms of learning, single-, double- and triple-loop, identified in this chapter are still subject to the purposes of the reflective process in the first instance. Knowledge, as we suggested before, and learning as we have seen here, may be disciplinary, technicist, dispositional or critical.

Conclusion

We identified earlier in this chapter a number of forms that reflection could take and indeed was taking on professional doctorate courses. These were: reflection-in-action as problem-solving; reflection on reflection-in-action; reflection on reflection-in-action which then leads to planned change to practice; reflection-in-action as the re-naming and re-framing of professional practice; intrinsic reflexive awareness in relation to identity; and extrinsic reflexive awareness in relation to action and situational constraint. Schon's (1983) powerful attack on technical rationality still has some resonances with the types of knowledge created by student-practitioners undertaking professional doctorate study. We have suggested here that ways of understanding reflective activity need to take account of both tacit workplace knowledge that allows the practitioner to 'go on' in the practicum and imported knowledge from outside. Furthermore, we have identified a range of focussed activity by the student-practitioner, and suggested that these foci in part determine the type of knowledge constructed by the student-practitioner and the type of reflection undertaken by them during the completion of their course. What is missing from this analysis is an understanding of those pedagogic and assessment processes which make up professional doctorate courses. It is to these matters that we now turn.

Part 3

Teaching and Learning

6

Marketing, Selection and Assessment

Introduction

In the previous chapters we have charted the development and growth of professional doctorates and considered the different forms of knowledge that are produced through the process of research in various domains of professional practice. In this chapter and the next we turn our attention to specific features of the 12 case-study programmes. Our concern here is to describe and understand similarity and difference both within and between the three subject areas covered by our sample. We clearly cannot claim that the 12 programmes we have selected represent the entire range of practice, though we have purposefully selected the programmes to encompass the range of practice within the three areas from our knowledge of those areas and earlier surveys of professional doctorates in England (Scott and Lunt 2000; Bourner *et al.* 2001a). Previous writing has tended to treat professional doctorates as a unity. Our contention is that, in order to understand the academic and professional implications of the development of professional doctorates, there is a need to examine in more detail the relationship between the characteristics of particular fields of professional practice and the emerging qualities of their related doctoral programmes. This requires us to make comparisons along a number of dimensions.

In this chapter we will look at the manner in which the programmes studied present themselves to their potential participants, how they select participants and how, in the course of the programme, they assess participants. This tells us about both the projected identities of the programmes and, closely related to this, the identities of the participants and graduates. The marketing of a programme acts to position it in relation to other programmes within a particular field. This positioning includes distinguishing the programme and the resulting qualification from other programmes and qualifications, and relating the programme, and its outcomes, to academic and professional practice. It tells potential participants both what to expect from the programme and who they, as participants and graduates, are, and who and what they could be, in relation to their field of practice. This process continues with the selection of participants, which identifies the key characteristics of those who can legitimately participate in the programme. The assessment of participants, including the processes of monitoring of progress through the programme, completes this process by formalizing what are the legitimate outcomes of the programme and how these outcomes can be recognized and evaluated. To trace this process, and to look at variation within and between the three different areas, we have drawn both on documents collected (including marketing material, prospectuses and course booklets) and the interviews with tutors, participants and graduates. Our concern here is not, however, with the motivations and aspirations of the participants nor with how they perceive the experience of doing and achieving a professional doctorate as relating to their professional trajectories. These issues will be addressed in Chapters 8 and 9.

Marketing professional doctorates

Amongst the material collected for each of the case-study programmes was promotional material, including leaflets about the courses and college prospectuses. These present each individual programme to potential participants and give them, and us as researchers, some insight into the characteristics of the intended target group and the projected relationship between the course offer and the requirements and desires of this group. From all the material collected, it is clear that the courses are *university* programmes (also a defining feature of the first generation of Australian professional doctorates, noted by Maxwell and Shanahan 2000).

A theme running through this chapter is the management of the tension between the organization and financing of a professional doctorate as a *university* programme and the underlying principle that, as a *professional* doctorate, there should be greater equity between the university, the profession and the workplace in the control of the processes and sanctioning of the products of the courses (see Lee *et al.* 2000). This tension is visible in the marketing of programmes. No matter what priority is given to notions of partnership and the importance of dialogue between academic and workplace agents, a professional doctorate programme is part of the formal offer of a university and its continuation, as such, is reliant upon meeting targets for fee-paying students and satisfaction of the quality assurance and enhancement procedures of the university. The description of the programme given in marketing material and in the prospectus thus locate the professional doctorate within a wider programme matrix on offer, differentiated in terms of, for instance, *place* in a structured sequence of programmes (running from undergraduate through taught postgraduate degrees to research degrees) and *position* in relation to a continuum running from vocational through to academic programmes. Whatever the rhetoric, the professional doctorate cannot, whilst it remains a university qualification, escape from university control. There is, however, some variation in how this control is achieved and realized within and between the types of programmes studied here.

There are, of course, resources on which universities can draw in marketing their programmes, whatever the level, subject or orientation of the course in question. What is of interest here, in relation to who the programme is intended to attract and how the relationship between the participant and the university is conceived, is which of these resources the university chooses to use in marketing a particular programme, and what distinct resources are provided by the programme in question, in this case one of a variety of forms of professional doctorate. The strategy to be adopted in presenting our analysis of this is to consider each form of doctorate in turn before considering commonalities and variations between the different areas.

In the marketing of the DBA programmes, a noticeable emphasis is given to the status of the university provider. One university, for instance, identifies itself as being a 'Top 20 research-led university'. Another draws attention to the prestige of its faculty and alumni, the competitiveness of its intake procedures and its track record in executive development. In establishing the prestige of the institution, there are two striking features. One is the prominence given to corporate and academic partnerships. The second is the prominence given to the international nature of these partnerships. One of the universities, for example, highlights its links with a prestigious European business school, another its international corporate partners.

Specialization in terms of sector of business administration did not appear to be crucial in the marketing of these programmes, with only one programme specifying a particular area of specialism, in this case a focus on the management of change in relation to new technology. In all cases a strong emphasis was placed on the DBA programme as a preparation for consultancy, or strengthening of existing consultancy practice. The programmes were thus not being presented as having an indexical relation with the labour market, but rather as building personal competence, skills and knowledge, and thus developing an increased personal capacity for consultancy work. This increased competence was a central focus for one of the programmes, with regular personal reflection on and auditing of competence throughout the programme. As would be expected, not all providers can lay claim to the prestige tag. In one case, the university placed emphasis on the productivity of entering an 'educational environment' in order to gain a doctoral level qualification that was relevant to professional practice and which facilitated the development of 'high level meta-cognitive and intellectual skills'. This is consonant with the general emphasis of DBA marketing on the development of personal skills and knowledge that can be deployed flexibly in the creative, shifting and uncertain world of consultancy. By placing emphasis on track record and prestige, programme providers demonstrated their awareness that enrolling on a DBA programme constituted for many participants a business investment, and therefore offered potential risk. As the participants and graduates of the programmes demonstrated in the interviews, a key factor in the selection of a particular programme was the maximizing of potential benefits and the minimizing of risk.

With respect to the DBA, it is not a matter of gaining specific skills and knowledge that are directly applied in the field of professional practice and which have a predictable and indexical relationship with performance. Whilst participants expect a benefit in terms of improved professional practice and/or professional prospects, they are aware that there is an element of risk involved, not least because the field of practice is prospective in orientation and unstable and unpredictable in its realization. The risk can be reduced by 'investing' in a known brand and in an organization with a track record of achievement in the field (partnerships and prestige faculty and alumni being indicators of achievement). The potential value of participation in doctoral level work and the development of a facility in research are clear to participants, and particularly cogent given the now well-established shift from a production based to knowledge economy. Business consultants and managers are clearly knowledge workers.

The academic standing of a university, and of a particular department within the university, is clearly also relevant in the marketing of EdD programmes. Participants in the programmes studied were overwhelmingly self-funding, were in full-time employment and were well established in their career in education and related areas. They had made careful decisions about the investment of time, effort and money in pursuing a doctorate. In presenting their EdD programme to potential participants, one university stated 'advance your career while you work by earning a doctorate from one of Britain's leading international universities'. The suggestion that the standing of the university is of importance to applicants is reinforced by reference to the rating of the department in the Research Assessment Exercise and the volume of research income. Another of the universities makes reference to the excellent research record, a vibrant research culture, internationally renowned scholars and strong networks.

Equally prominent in the course descriptions, and mentioned by participants as a key factor in their selection of a programme, are the issues of choice and flexibility. All the universities point to the ability of the programme to be adapted to meet both professional needs and personal circumstances. One programme, for instance, states that it has the flexibility 'to cater for your lifestyle, to fit with your work and family commitments' and makes it possible 'to choose how you wish to study, and the direction you wish to go, at a pace that suits you'.

Career relevance is also an issue. In the cases studied, this is presented as relating to keeping abreast of current research and development in the field and the development or refinement of research skills. As with the DBA programmes, there is no direct articulation with career development. The EdD programmes are not offering a range of necessary skills or knowledge that are the prerequisites for a particular change in direction or career development. Unlike the marketing of DBA programmes, little is made of the development of particular professional competences, nor is much made of partnerships with other institutions. The EdD is presented more as offering research skills and the opportunity to reflect on professional practice both through the conduct of professionally relevant research and contact with up to the minute theory, research and development in the field of education. In this, the excellence of the teaching offered in the programme is highlighted in two of the cases, as might be expected in programmes being run by educationalists, for educationalists.

Like the DBA, little is made of the specialist orientation of the EdD programmes. Whilst options are offered within the programmes (for instance, in the management of education, special educational needs and the teaching of English to speakers of other languages), these are presented as indicators of the flexibility and relevance of the programme, rather than the creation of a specialized identity within the field or the acquisition of segmental expertise. Strong identification with a particular phase, sector of professional practice, theoretical perspective or disciplinary specialization appears neither to be central to the marketing of EdD programmes nor the selection of programmes by participants. In the participant accounts, more localized criteria appear to be at play, for instance the proximity of the university to their home or workplace, or prior professional or academic contact with a particular department or individual. Whilst there are clear differences in the marketing of EdD and DBA programmes, the EngD programmes stand out from both along a number of dimensions. The programmes are, as we have seen, designed to meet a particular perceived need within engineering generally, and within particular sectors of industry in particular. Partnership with industry, and, for each programme, with a particular sector within industry, is a key feature of the design of the EngD initiative and unsurprisingly features heavily in the marketing of the programmes. All the courses studied list their key industrial partners and stress that they are in a unique position to serve their particular sector of industry, for instance, the steel industry. This specialization means that the facilities offered by universities and the specialized expertise of staff also feature strongly. That the university was chosen, and the programme endorsed, by the national funding council (ESPRC) and that scholarships and sponsorships are available to participants, are also a central feature of the marketing. In addition, mention is made of the quality of teaching and quality and track record in fundamental and applied research.

The EngD programmes make direct appeal to the career aspirations of potential participants. The literature on the programmes state that they are intended for 'aspiring chief executives', that as multi-disciplinary programmes combining engineering research expertise with management training and workplace experience they provide the required skills and knowledge for a 'successful career in industry' and a 'fast track into senior management'. Whilst these programmes are able to accommodate participants who are already established in an engineering career (and some programmes actively seek such people through their industrial partnerships), recent young graduates comprise the majority of each programme intake. The potential benefits of the form of education offered by the EngD programmes are clearly visible to these graduates. Entry is highly competitive, and the sectoral nature of programmes makes selection of a programme by a potential participant heavily dependent upon area of specialism.

Selection of participants

It is in the setting of formal entry requirements that the control of the university is most clear. As McWilliam *et al.* (2002) have pointed out, any threat to the status of the doctorate, as the most prestigious higher education qualification, constitutes a major challenge to the reputation of a university. A perceived 'softening' in doctoral entry requirements, or in assessment requirements, could undermine the standing of the university's offer as a whole. It is unsurprising, then, that the academic entry requirements for the professional doctorate programmes studied at least match those of the PhD, and in most cases exceed them. There are, however, differences within and between the types of doctorate studied here.

All the DBA programmes require an MBA, or other masters or equivalent, plus management experience. In one case a 'good' masters in a 'relevant discipline' is required. In two cases, the type of management experience required is related to the areas covered by the programme (for instance, one programme requires three years of relevant leadership experience) and the expertise of staff available to supervise. There is a range within the DBA programmes from highly competitive admission, with an elaborate selection process that reduces around 100 applicants to a cohort of 20, through to relatively inclusive admission once the basic requirements are met. One programme, for instance, includes an initial screening which includes a review of each applicant's competences, evaluation of referees' comments and an assessment of whether appropriate support for the proposed research is available. This is followed by an interview with the Director of Studies and a specialist tutor in the area of the proposed research. The final decision is ratified by a university committee. In another of the programmes, applicants have to produce a statement about the proposed research and how this links to the main themes of the programme.

In all cases a clear distinction is made, both by tutors in the interview and in the literature, between the predominantly skills orientation of the MBA and the research orientation of the DBA. Whilst the MBA *reproduces* management knowledge, which is acquired by course participants, the DBA *produces* management knowledge, and programme participants both benefit from this and acquire the capability to conduct applied research and produce 'real world' knowledge. There is thus a relatively clear progression from masters to doctoral level work. This distinction is confirmed in the interviews, in which tutors state that they would not expect MBA graduates to have received any form of research training, and participants and graduates note that they had little idea about the principles of the design and conduct of research before starting the DBA programme.

Of the three types of doctorate, the DBA programmes are most explicit about non-standard entry. To enable overseas and other candidates without a recognized degree to be included, two of the universities set an indicative Graduate Management Admission Test (GMAT) score, as well as setting threshold International English Language Testing System (IELTS) and Test of English as a Foreign Language (TOEFL) scores. Whilst a relevant post-graduate qualification and appropriate professional experience (or equiva-lent) are required for admission to each of the four DBA programmes, a different relationship between undergraduate study, postgraduate qualifica-tions and professional experience is presented by the EdD admission requirements. Three of the four EdD programmes state that entrants must be graduates with a UK or equivalent degree. In one case it is stated that this must be 'a good honours degree and/or masters degree'. Another states a preference for an upper second class degree, and states that most applicants have a masters degree. The third states that, in addition to the degree, appli-cants will normally be expected to possess an 'advanced qualification in education'.

These three examples indicate a certain amount of ambiguity about the relationship between masters and other advanced level study in education and the education doctorate. Education masters vary in the degree to which they are directly practice oriented, provide a disciplinary perspective on education or provide a preparation for research in education. From the admissions requirements of these EdDs it is difficult to see what, in the way of preparation for doctoral work, the masters degree is providing. It is the level of the first degree that appears to be providing an indication of the academic attainment of the participants. The masters degree is indicating a specific academic interest in education, though the content and orientation of this degree covers a wide range. The relationship between professional experi-ence and the masters degree in education is also ambiguous. There is not the same articulation between career development and a masters level qualifica-tion as there is in business and management, where the MBA has a clear practical orientation and brings tangible career advantages. This also brings a degree of ambiguity to the relationship between the EdD and professional experience. None of the four courses studied require extended professional experience. Experience (set at three years in two cases) is either 'normal' or 'taken into consideration'.

The fourth EdD programme gives considerably more detail with regard to admissions requirements. Here an attempt is made to articulate the EdD with other postgraduate programmes in education offered by the university, and to define what can be counted as equivalent to this. It is also more explicit about the criteria that have to be met by the required research proposal. A successful proposal: 'demonstrates reflection on the relationship between theory and practice in education; exhibits a high level of critical analysis; gives evidence of ability to select and apply appropriate research methods; and shows the potential to make a significant contribution to the theory and practice of education'.

All the EngD programmes require a first or upper second at UK honours or equivalent level. One states that over two-thirds of the previous year's entrants had a first-class degree. These requirements bear the closest resemblance to minimum expectations for a PhD. Given that the EngD is designed to provide entry to a profession, it is more likely that applicants will be coming directly from undergraduate study, and will have neither a postgraduate qualification nor substantial professional experience. This was confirmed in interviews with EngD staff and students, although all promotional material expressed a strong preference for applicants with some years of industrial experience. Amongst the participants and graduates interviewed, there was a mixture of those with a masters degree and those with just a first degree, and those with industrial experience and those without.

Entry to the EngD, because of its track record in providing an effective route to employment and subsequent fast-track promotion, and because it attracts enhanced financial support for participants, was seen as highly competitive. Participants had made a positive decision to take what they saw as a challenging, high status and potentially rewarding programme, at least on a par with a PhD, if not superior in terms of career prospects and more competitive. This view of the EngD was shared by tutors associated with the programme and by participants and graduates. One of the industrial partners interviewed, however, expressed concern that, whilst he saw the EngD as excellent preparation for engineering management, many colleagues were uncertain about the status of the degree in comparison to the PhD. His concern that employers do not understand what an EngD is and how it differs from a PhD is echoed by some of the participants. Of the period spent working on his industrial project one participant observes:

> the main thing I think I've found with the project is there's not a lot of people out there in the real world who actually know what an EngD is or what it's about.

Similarly, another participant on the same programme states:

> I always have to explain what it is and they'll say, 'Oh, it's like a PhD then', which it is, obviously, you know, but it's, there's more to it than that; and perhaps that's not appreciated.

The EngD programmes were the only ones in the sample that involved professionals (usually representatives of their industrial partners) in the selection process. In all other cases, selection was solely in the hands of the university.

Assessment and the monitoring of progress

The marketing of a programme and the selection process act to delineate the characteristics of the participants in the programme. This therefore both marks out the orientation of the programme and the range of possible identities for its participants. Assessment plays a key role here, in that the processes of assessment, through the identification of a range of possible legitimate outcomes, act to sanction particular identities. Marketing and selection determine who can legitimately participate; assessment marks out the range of possible characteristics of the graduates from the programmes.

From our earlier discussion of the development and growth of professional doctorates in various domains of practice, we have seen that one of the key features that distinguishes them from the conventional PhD in the UK is that most include components that are taught and assessed and that contribute to the overall award of the doctorate. Whilst it is now common for UK PhD programmes to include compulsory taught components that are assessed, the final award rests solely on the examination of the thesis. In contrast, all 12 of the professional doctorate programmes we studied included assessed components other than a thesis, which contributed to the examination and award of the doctorate. As with the other aspects of the programmes considered thus far, there is variation both within and between programme types.

Across the programmes studied, assessment takes place in different stages of the course, serves different purposes and takes a variety of forms. Maxwell (2003b), in discussing Seddon's (2000) distinction between first and second generation professional doctorates in Australia, draws attention to the move from a coursework plus thesis pattern of assessment to portfolio-based assessment as one element in the production of new forms of professional doctorate, and one indicator of a shift away for the domination of the concerns of the academy. Of the three examples of second generation professional doctorates discussed by Maxwell, only one has adopted a portfolio as an alternative to the coursework plus thesis pattern. Whilst only one of the programmes in our sample of 12 has adopted portfolio-based assessment, a number of others have departed significantly from a simple coursework plus thesis arrangement.

The culmination of all the DBA programmes studied is the presentation of a piece of research that makes a contribution to knowledge in the field. There is variation, however, in the form in which this research is presented, the nature of the other pieces of assessed work and the relationship of the pieces of work to each other. There was also distinct variation in the strength and formality of the monitoring of progress through the programme. None of the cases could be described as adhering strictly to a coursework plus thesis pattern. In the two cases where a substantial thesis is the prime focus of the assessment of the programme, the assessment of courses is indirect and developmental in form. In the two cases where individual courses are assessed, the mode of presentation of the research component of the course is more flexible (two short reports in one case, and the option of a portfolio instead of a thesis in the other).

One of the thesis-oriented programmes takes a strong professional development perspective on the progress of participants through the programme.

At the centre of the monitoring process is an initial audit of professional competences and from this the construction of a development plan. This includes the agreement of targets by participants and their academic advisors. These are reviewed each year as part of the annual assessment of progress. To move to the thesis stage of the programme, each participant has to produce evidence that they have met the professional competence targets set. In addition, participants have to attend all mandatory sessions, which include research training workshops, and produce a working paper of a publishable standard, a critique of a relevant thesis and an approved research proposal. This gives the whole process a strong professional and personal orientation, whilst maintaining a distinct overall research focus. The mode of evaluation of professional competence sanctions reflection on professional practice and self-evaluation in dialogue with colleagues and academic advisers, who themselves have strong professional experience and good links with professional practice. All elements of this first stage of the course must be passed in order to move to the second stage of the programme. The research related to the thesis is the focus of this second stage. The assessment of the second stage, and ultimately of the degree, centres on the examination of a thesis of between 45,000 and 80,000 words. Participants also have to produce two papers of publishable quality, which further stresses the need to relate the research to a wider community.

There is a clear distinction in this programme between the initial, foundational stage and the subsequent research-based stage. The mode of monitoring and assessment focuses on the development of the professional and research competence of the individual rather than on course content. A similar split is made in the other thesis-oriented DBA programme, but with a greater focus on the development of the research project and less directly on the competences of the individual. The compulsory core of workshops is not directly assessed. Oral and written presentations on the research proposal and design are required, as is a full literature review (to be judged of publishable standard) and a report and oral presentation of a pilot study. Here the courses and the assessments that mark the progress of the participant through the programme are seen as supporting the production of the thesis at the end of the programme. Again, it should be noted that the assessments are predominantly developmental and that there is an emphasis on verbal presentation to peers and the production of publishable written work.

Neither of the two DBA programmes that assess the taught components of the course more directly (for example, through essays of 4–5000 words) requires a substantial thesis. In one case, two short research projects are produced, each of around 20,000 words. In the other, either a 'dissertation' of 40–50,000 words or a portfolio of 'equivalent length and standard' is submitted. In these two cases there is stronger regulation of the taught part of the programme with a marked departure from the conventional PhD like thesis. What is clear from the assessment and monitoring practices of the DBA is that whilst there is a very clear emphasis on research and the development of research skills and dispositions in the programmes, there is a wide range of forms of assessment practice. The distinction made between coursework followed by thesis and portfolio forms of assessment is not sufficiently subtle to describe these cases and illuminate the different orientation of the programmes. It is, however, difficult to argue that a departure from a more conventional assessment regime signifies a shift of control away from the interests of the academy towards those of the profession or the workplace. The most marked shift amongst the DBA programmes studied appears to be away from predetermined sets of research competences, of the sort specified by the Economic and Social Research Council, for instance (see ESRC 2001), towards the negotiation between participant and supervisor of professional and personal competences relating to the development of research capability. This can be seen as being in accord with the objective to develop skills and knowledge appropriate to consultancy in a field such as business and management, which is in constant flux and demands creativity. It is clear from our interviews that tutors, participants and graduates appreciate this; a marked contrast to the prescription of required research skills.

The coursework plus thesis assessment structure is much stronger amongst the EdD programmes studied. In all four cases a sequential structure has been adopted, with a clearly marked transition between the taught part of the programme and the conduct of research. In one case, the first part of the EdD programme consists of masters level courses, and participants can seek exemption from this if they have an appropriate masters level qualification. This must be recognized as providing the basis for the production of a research proposal; there is a transitional module for candidates whose qualifications do not meet this criterion. The subsequent, second part of the programme is focussed very clearly on the production of the thesis, but is still divided into two phases. The first focuses on the production of a 15,000 word report comprising a literature review and reflection on initial research. This is formally assessed and has to be passed in order to move to the second phase in which a thesis of 40,000 to 50,000 words is produced.

In the other three cases, transition is achieved by passing an array of individually assessed taught modules (variously five, six and eight modules) and the approval of a research proposal. In each case the taught modules comprise a mixture of research methods and substantive modules. The modules are all individually assessed by essays, varying in length between 3000 and 6000 words.

All the programmes studied have a substantial, conventionally defined thesis, varying in length between 30,000 and 50,000 words. The following statement from one of the programmes can be taken to represent the broad expectations of the thesis or dissertation, which:

> will represent a contribution to knowledge which shows evidence of originality and independence, critical evaluation of the appropriate literature, research skills and the ability to communicate the results and their implications in clear English. It is expected that the results of

dissertations will be worthy of being, and in many cases will actually be, published. Your dissertation will be assessed by internal and external examiners and will normally involve a viva voce examination.

Another states that:

The Research Thesis is a major element of the EdD programme. It is a student-driven independent, research-based investigation which must provide evidence of originality and independent critical ability and must contain matter suitable for publication. The thesis is expected to make a contribution to academic and professional knowledge and understanding.

From these descriptions it is difficult to distinguish expectations of the thesis from a PhD thesis. It is notable that all the EdD tutors interviewed expressed concern about the clarity with which differences between the EdD and the PhD is defined and the extent to which examiners appreciated the differences in expectations between a PhD thesis and an EdD thesis. For instance, one tutor stated:

when I was the programme director, I used to try and make sure that I didn't have, if it could possibly be avoided, two people examining [who were] inexperienced examiners in EdD. So, if I had an external that had never done it with us before, then I would want an internal who had done several because I know, from acting as an internal examiner, if someone's coming as an external who has never done an EdD before, then actually their big question is, 'so, what's the difference here? How are we, how are we going to judge this?'

This tutor stressed that whilst the EdD thesis must be coherent and rigorous, and make a contribution to knowledge, it is likely to be more limited in scope, especially with respect to the literature reviewed and the extent of the empirical work. Whilst the professional focus of the EdD thesis is mentioned, much anxiety is expressed about the danger of examiners failing to recognize the distinctiveness of the shorter EdD thesis and judging it as failing to meet expectations developed from examining PhD theses in education. That many PhD theses in education are produced by experienced practitioners and have a professional focus, clearly contributes to this problem. Some tutors themselves appeared to be uncertain of the difference:

I have my slight problems with the parity of esteem. I guess, call it snobbism, call it association, but the line that we've taken is, the criteria for the thesis are exactly the same for the EdD as they are for the PhD. The crunch words are originality and independent critical thought and the examination form is the same. It's got the same headings. And the upgrade is the same. I mean, there is a massive issue about whether you can do certain things within, as it was, forty thousand words. And people typically were going over forty thousand words.

In other univeresities this had also been an issue of concern for tutors, as one course leader illustrates:

> I would be quite interested actually to look at the difference between this doctorate and PhDs because it did become an issue of contention. Some of the people who had started working as tutor-supervisors very early on in the programme before [the previous course leader] took over, did have this sort of feeling that the doctorate was a slightly lower standard or an inferior degree or, I'm not quite sure. I haven't actually got my head round what they thought but, and they were quite shocked. I would say in fact, it is a doctorate of a very high standard.

Yet another course leader states that when developing their EdD programme there had been:

> quite a lot of reflection about exactly how this is going to develop from what we expect from PhDs and there was quite a lot of discussion about it. I'm not sure we have any hard and fast answers and I'm not sure that there is any absolutely clear difference from what we should expect from a PhD apart from slightly shorter maybe.

Of the three programme areas, it is interesting to note that it is education in which the programme structures and assessment practices are the most conservative. It is also where there are the greatest anxieties about the relationship between the PhD and the professional doctorate, the tightest regulation of the boundary between taught and research components and the greatest ambiguity in the relationship between masters and doctoral level work.

Business, education and engineering as areas of study within higher education are all in some respect multi-disciplinary. Higher education programmes in business and education will, for example, draw on theory and research in sociology and psychology. Similarly, engineering programmes will draw variously on fundamental theory and research, for instance, in physics and chemistry. The three areas being studied could thus, in Bernstein's (2000) terms, be considered regions of knowledge, each of which addresses a particular area of human, social or scientific practice. Of the three doctoral programmes being studied here, it is only the EngD, however, that sets out explicitly to bring together two established regions of knowledge in the production of individuals with a particular array of skills and knowledge to address a perceived need within the field of practice. Whilst the doctoral programmes in education and business will bring participants into contact with recontextualized sociology and psychology, without the necessity or intention of creating sociologists and psychologists, in the same way doctoral courses in engineering will include recontextualized physics and chemistry without the necessity or intention of creating physicists and chemists. The EngD brings together the academic cultures of business and engineering in the production of the research engineer. We will discuss this in greater detail in the following chapter when considering curriculum content and pedagogy. What is important here is that the manner in which different regions of knowledge come into play in the production of research engineers, and the part played by workplace settings in this process, give a very different character to the monitoring of progress and assessment of participants.

The stress placed on the development and application of skills and knowledge in workplace settings has three interrelated implications. First, the competences required by participants will by necessity extend beyond the academic sphere and will include, for instance, a range of personal, interpersonal and communication skills. Second, the ability of participants to apply this diverse range of skills and knowledge needs to be assessed to meet the objectives of the programmes. Third, the conditions and contexts within which participants are assessed must thus be diverse and extend beyond the university and its usual assessment practices.

In all four of the EngD programmes detailed attention is given to providing explicit statements of the competences which participants will be required to demonstrate. This provides in each case a clear framework for assessment of the taught part of the programme and substantial attention is paid in all programmes to targeting and assessing these competences and the ability to apply related engineering and business knowledge. One result of this is a marked variation in the levels and forms of assessment within programmes. In one programme, for instance, highly targeted assessments are built into modules with weekly written tests set in the first year of the university-based engineering programme as part of a cycle of lectures and lab-based tasks. These tests must be passed for participants to progress through the programme. Later assessments are broader in scope and involve work in university and industrial settings and extended presentations to academic and professional audiences. The other programmes similarly incorporate written exams, coursework, individual and team projects, case studies, journals and portfolios.

How the assessed elements are related to each other varies between the engineering programmes. One, for instance, incorporates an entire Diploma in Management. Each module is assessed as it would in a stand-alone course, and all modules have to be passed for the candidate to proceed to complete the EngD degree. Other elements of the taught programme have their own independent assessments. In contrast, another of the programmes draws all assessments together in a portfolio that is developed over the course of the programme. Each component of the programme has assessed post-module work to be completed, and this goes into the portfolio, alongside the work relating to the development and outcomes of an industry-based research project.

All the EngD programmes have clear procedures for periodic review and the monitoring of progress. All require some form of report to be produced by the participant at the end of each year. In one case, it is the participant who has to convene the meeting, seen as part of the development of their professional competence. There is a common use of oral as well as written reporting and presentation to both academic and professional audiences, again as a way of testing and extending professional competences seen as essential for research engineers. As with the other professional doctorates, research is an essential component of the EngD programme. Although the taught component of all the programmes is substantial (constituting two-thirds of the total required credits in one case), all programmes state that research is the main focus. In three of the programmes, a major research project is presented in thesis form. The criteria by which the thesis is judged retain the need to contribute to the production of knowledge, but place this in an applied industrial context. As stated in the assessment criteria for one of these programmes, the candidate has to demonstrate through the thesis:

> An ability to assimilate and assess existing knowledge; to add to the body of applied engineering by undertaking and communicating the results of research in a systematic and ordered manner; to appreciate fully the potential of their research in its wider economic, social, technical and environmental contexts.

It is also stated that a fifth of the thesis must address commercial and business aspects of the research.

In the fourth programme, the research conducted is presented as the major part of a portfolio. The portfolio must demonstrate teamwork and leadership skills, project management skills, oral and written communication skills, technical organization skills, financial engineering project planning and control, expert engineering knowledge, application of skills and knowledge in new situations, ability to seek optimal solutions to multi-faceted engineering problems and ability to search out relevant information sources. The portfolio also contains a profile listing all modules taken and marks achieved, and indicates how proficiency in all required competencies has been demonstrated. Although the candidate is assessed through the portfolio as a whole, only one element of this enters the public domain. This is an 'innovation report', which can take the form of a mini thesis of 50–80 pages, that documents changes that have taken place and demonstrates where value has been added by the work carried out.

It is notable that both the supervision and examination of the research conducted involves both academics and professionals. In all programmes a panel of academic and industrial partners oversees the development and conduct of the research. Similarly, an expert panel of academics and professionals assesses the thesis or portfolio. A common feature of the examination is a substantial, for example, 45-minute, oral presentation of the research by the candidate to a mixed industrial and academic audience.

Conclusion

From our discussion of the marketing of the case-study programmes, the manner in which participants are selected and the ways in which participants' progress is monitored and outputs assessed, it is clear that these professional doctorates are distinctly different from conventional PhDs in their corresponding areas. It is also clear that there are significant differences between the three areas of knowledge and professional practice covered by our sample.

Unsurprisingly, all the programmes make an appeal to potential participants who have an interest in the development of professional practice and in their own professional development. Whereas a PhD is primarily aimed at those who want to pursue a research career, or to teach in higher education, the professional doctorates attempt to relate research to a wider range of possibilities for professional advancement and development. The establishment of a distinct identity for professional doctorates becomes increasingly important as PhDs become more structured and increasingly have a substantial taught component. In the three areas covered here, this is even more of an imperative as each region of knowledge has a close relationship with professional practice, and therefore PhDs in these areas will frequently address questions of direct relevance to professional practice.

In the marketing of the DBA and the EdD, there is a clear acknowledgement of the demanding professional circumstances of potential participants and efforts are made to demonstrate that the programmes can accommodate these. In presenting the EdD to potential applicants, the flexibility of the programmes sometimes takes a higher profile than the content. An important factor in marketing the DBA appeared to be the prestige of the university. The EngD, on the other hand, was presented as universally of high standing, but differentiated in terms of the sector of engineering practice addressed, and this was reflected in the specialism of the university or department and the industrial partners involved.

All programmes have demanding selection criteria, and in some cases they are more demanding than for a PhD in the same area. The criteria further reinforce the emerging identity of the 'researching practitioner'. The relationship between the form and content of the programmes in the three areas and the potential utility of the doctorate to participants and graduates varies across the areas covered, something we will take up and explore further in the next chapter.

The programmes draw on a range of assessment and monitoring practices. The EngD programmes use the widest range, appearing to select the form of assessment on the basis of fitness for purpose. The EdD is surprisingly the most conservative in terms of assessment practice, perhaps related to the lack of clarity of the relationship between the EdD and other professional and academic qualifications and a perceived lack of confidence in the relationship between research and professional practice in education. In all cases, the form the assessment takes, and the criteria used, act to shape and relay the characteristics of the legitimate outcomes of the programme and therefore the sanctioned identities. A key question in understanding the transformative potential of professional doctorates is thus, 'whose criteria?', a question we address in the last chapter.

It is clear that, certainly within our sample, professional doctorates have, to varying degrees, moved away from the initial 'first generation' coursework plus thesis model of assessment, though as we shall see in the following chapter this still exerts a distinct influence on the structuring of programmes. Few, however, have moved towards the portfolio forms of assessment identified by Maxwell (2003b) as exemplifying 'second generation' professional doctorates. Ultimately, it appears from our sample, the university retains control over what counts as acceptable outputs at doctoral level, and therefore continues to regulate the principles, and agents, of the production and reproduction of knowledge. The strength of regulation with respect to professional contexts does, however, vary as we have seen here by looking across the three types of professional doctorate. An important factor appears to be the positioning of the particular region of knowledge with respect to both disciplinary knowledge and professional practice. In the following chapter we take up this and related issues when addressing the content of the professional doctorate programmes and how this is organized, *and* the forms of pedagogy adopted and the pedagogic relations (re)produced. In other words, we examine the 'what' and the 'how' of the programmes.

7

Curriculum and Pedagogy

Introduction

This chapter deals with questions relating to what is taught and learnt in the various professional doctorate programmes that we studied – the skills, knowledge and dispositions that constitute the curriculum; and how this is taught and learnt – the practices, processes and relations that constitute pedagogy. As we have observed earlier, previous research and writing on professional doctorates has either focussed on the specific characteristics of professional doctorates in comparison to more conventional PhD programmes (for example Maxwell and Shanahan 1997, 2000; Bourner *et al.* 2001a), or has taken the growth of professional doctorates as an indicator of a shift in modes of the production of knowledge.

As with the previous chapters, the analysis of the curriculum and pedagogy presented here differs from previous work in two key respects. First, by looking in detail at a range of professional doctorates, we are able to explore similarities and differences within and between different forms of professional doctorate. Second, for each of the cases studied, a variety of forms of data representing different perspectives and positions are analysed. In addressing the question of the organizational features of the programmes studied, curriculum content and the pedagogic strategies and relations, we have analysed published and unpublished information about the programmes (including prospectuses and course material), interviews with tutors working on the programmes and interviews with participants and graduates from the programmes. Whilst previous studies have tended to homogenize professional doctorates, this study is able to present both the distinctive character of the professional doctorate and to explore difference within and between particular domains of practice in relation to both the institutions, forms of partnership and academic disciplines involved and the characteristics, motivations and workplace circumstances of the participants.

Programme structure

In the previous chapter we explored the different forms and patterns of assessment employed by the 12 programmes studied. We were able to relate these to the projected identities of the programmes, the relationship between the professional doctorate qualification and the field of professional practice, and the officially sanctioned identities of the participants. In considering the pattern of assessment we noted that there was some departure from the established coursework plus thesis structure of the taught doctorate. Aside from signifying the relative importance of the taught and research elements, the structure of the programme lays out the temporal and spatial framework within which the elements of the curriculum are organized. Limitations on the time and resources available mean that curricular decisions have to be made within this pedagogic economy. These decisions lead, for instance, to the prioritization of particular skills and knowledge, made visible through the different weightings of the various components of each programme. They can also reveal assumptions made about the participants in the programmes and about the form of academic and professional knowledge and the relations between these forms of knowledge.

At the most fundamental level, there are differences between the programmes with respect to the amount of 'pedagogic time' available. All the EngD programmes are full-time, and take four years to complete, with one programme offering the possibility of reduction of the length of the programme for participants with approved MSc or MBA qualifications. This is one year longer than a comparable PhD programme and allows for additional content, such as the incorporation of a substantial proportion of an MBA programme, industrial placements and other supporting activities, such as a European study tour in one of the programmes. All four of the programmes are heavily timetabled, and very demanding of participants in terms of time commitment, on and off campus. As the course leader for one of the programmes stated, the EngD is an intensive and demanding programme and 'is not for the faint-hearted'.

In contrast, the DBA and EdD programmes are offered principally as part-time courses. All the DBA courses are part-time, with just one being open to full-time participants. In each case the ethos of the programme stresses the close relationship between the programme and professional practice. Unlike the EngD, the DBA does not offer professional experience; it is the participants' everyday workplace experience that underwrites the professional relevance of the doctorate. The length of period of study varies between three and five years. The three-year programme is split into one year of taught courses and two years focusing on research; the five-year programme into two years of taught courses and three years research. In comparison with the EngD, the amount of contact time is small on these programmes – two, for instance, work on a six-week cycle of preparation, weekend workshops and follow-up in the taught part of the programme. These two courses offer between 72 and 96 hours per year total group contact time, a small fraction of the contact time on the EngD programmes. The strength of insulation between the taught and the research-based elements of the programmes also varies, as we have seen in our discussion of assessment in the DBA programme.

Three of the four EdD programmes were offered in both part-time and full-time modes. The fourth was a distance-learning programme offered only on a part-time basis. The shortest of the programmes was three years part-time, with background work to the research being done in the first year, leading to the research project in the second and third years. The other programmes had a modular structure, with the taught courses in the first part of the programme (two years part-time) moving into the thesis related work in the second part of the programme (two or three years part-time). In all cases there is a threshold to be crossed, for instance, passing module assessments and having a research proposal approved, between the taught elements and the research based phase. All programmes have some form of collective activity in the second phase of the programme to maintain the cohort effect established in the first phase of the programme. The minimum period of registration of part-time students on these programmes is four years in two cases and five years in one. The minimum period of full-time registration is three years in all cases.

One of the notable features of all the courses studied is the 'cohort effect'. Working together as a group in the taught parts of the programme produces strong peer support networks. All the programmes attempted to extend this into the research-based part of the course by organizing group workshops, seminars and/or conferences for participants while they were engaged in conducting their own research. This was clearly appreciated by the participants, and for many of the interviewees had been a key factor in choosing to do a professional doctorate rather than a conventional PhD. This cohort effect differs in strength and form between the programme types, however. The work on the EngD is intensive and full-time, and the relationships between the participants appear to be more akin to those within a taught masters programme. Even so, they expressed appreciation of the mutual support provided by the university-based cohort during their industrial placements and off-campus research work. The DBA and EdD students are all practising professionals with varying degrees of overlap in experience and interests. Participants saw the peer support as being vital in maintaining motivation and sharing common experiences and problems as 'researching professionals', as well as debating academic issues and discussing areas of common professional interest. One EdD student stressed the importance of being able to engage with people from other areas of professional practice and debate fundamental differences in perspectives:

> The clashes we get in debate of different paradigms. That's one of the big things that's come out of debating. People who are not in education

for instance, who come from the medical world and from business. So we have different orientations and different paradigms of working. And you get in here and it's just chucking yourself around and it's really arguing our ground for taking a particular methodology or whatever.

Other EdD participants indicate that they value coming into contact with others from different phases and sectors of education:

I really like it, actually, because I think we've kind of come together and bonded. And I've appreciated the, I guess, the experiences of people from all realms of Education because I don't get it otherwise.

This experience of working together with peers is seen by many as being a valued feature of the pedagogic approach of the EdD, as these two comments from participants illustrate:

Our group seems to have gelled very well and it's a diverse group, and we have debate and lots of different views can contribute to that and always it is good and I think people appreciate, well I certainly appreciate, that style. A colleague of mine is doing a Masters, a straight Masters in research methods, but it's a very didactic approach to research methods and I wouldn't want to go through that again to be perfectly honest.

A couple of days away from work, away from home, with a group of people that I've always got on very well with, very supportive. We have our own network outside of the EdD weekends. We went out last night for a meal. . . . You know, we do, we're very supportive. And that, really, as I said at the beginning, was one of the things that attracted me to the EdD in the first place. And that is very much how I prefer to work and wanted to do it.

Similarly, DBA students valued the support provided by working in a group or cohort. As with the EdD, this provided both support and motivation as indicated by this comment from a DBA graduate:

Nine years after we started, I'm still in touch with a number of those people. Being part of a group. I didn't like it sometimes, this is an awful thing to say, I didn't like it sometimes when other people seemed to be making more progress than me. It was kind of, it would spur me on. There was a very, very good sharing environment so when people got, you know, particular texts or, you know, sources of information or whatever.

In all the EdD and DBA programmes, the examined taught component and the research-based component were sequential, with progress to the research component being dependent, at least in part, on successful completion of the taught component. In the EngD programmes, which are by design multi-disciplinary and bring together research training in a specialized area of engineering with management education and the acquisition of a range of generic skills, the temporal division between taught and research components was less clear cut. In only one case was a strongly sequential mode of organization adopted. In all others, the research component of the degree ran in parallel with the taught components. In addition, there was an interweaving of the university and workplace components and of the engineering, management and generic skills taught components of the EngD programmes. Thus, although different departments or units within the university delivered these components, a strong sense of the interrelationship between academic research in engineering and practice in industrial and commercial settings was achieved, and this was reflected in the comments made by programme participants and graduates. For example, one graduate observes:

> So, I know the academic side of, say, a mathematical application, something like numerical analysis. But, in isolation, that's of no relevance. Equally, there's no point of a pure industrialist knowing about it, because he [sic] wouldn't know what to do with it. He wouldn't know how to apply it. Whereas I've actually sort of done the theory side and applied it in real practice.

Others commented on the interplay between the technical and management aspects of the programme:

> [The management courses] were very good from the point of view of I had a very technical background and I knew nothing about the way business is operated, about management, so I broadened enormously from that point of view in my understanding of how the whole engineering business operates. Meeting with lots of people in industry, that was great, that was really very enjoyable.

One graduate reflects on how bringing together engineering and management has had an unexpectedly profound and enduring effect:

> I knew I was interested in it but I don't think I realised quite what a dramatic effect it was going to have on my outlook on things. And certainly working here, my line manager said to me a couple of times, you know, he goes, 'You don't behave like a PhD', from his experience of having people working for him before.

The delivery of the taught components of the programmes was in all cases segmental, that is content is divided into small units. The size, duration and mode of delivery varied greatly across the programmes. In one EdD programme, for instance, each unit comprised two consecutive days' input, with few interdictions on the order in which participants took the units. Other modes of organization included intensive one-week blocks distributed across the year and bringing together a geographically dispersed group of participants. Variation in the form of organization of the content of the courses had implications for the cohesiveness of the programme, the extent to which participants felt themselves to be part of a cohort and the manner in which university-based work could be related to day-to-day professional practice. Whilst various patterns of attendance were adopted by the part-time courses, all provide some form of periodic intensive experience, ranging from two days to one week.

Curriculum content

The EngD courses are notable for the breadth of content. Each programme is based on an analysis of the skills and knowledge required to be a research engineer. This, as we have seen, brings together substantive knowledge and skills in management and a specialist area of engineering plus a range of specific and generic workplace related skills. The programmes differ with respect to the balance between the management and the engineering components of the programme. In one case almost double the number of hours are given to management than to engineering. At the other extreme, another course is dominated by engineering input, with management training restricted to a small number of weekend workshops and activities that are viewed as supporting the main programme. The manner in which the balance between content areas changes as the participant progresses through the programme also varies. In one case, engineering dominates in the first year with an equal balance between engineering and management training in the second year and a shift towards management and professional issues alongside workplace-based research in the third and fourth years. In another of the programmes, management dominates in the early part of the programme with a progressive shift over time to engineering and workplace focussed project work.

All the EngD programmes maintain a clear academic division of labour between management and engineering. In all cases, the management components of the course are designed and delivered by the university business school or equivalent. Usually this is in the form of a part of a Diploma or MBA programme. The strong insulation between the management and engineering components is facilitated by the identification of the competences required by research engineers in both areas of knowledge and practice. The division of labour and the determination of content are thus instrumentally driven. In the interviews, tutors stated that they experienced very little tension between the management and engineering components of the programmes, though their affiliation to one or other was often made clear. This partnership between regions of knowledge appears to be facilitated by a clear sense of shared purpose. It should also be noted that there is a distinct difference in the levels at which study is taking place. The knowledge being produced, in most cases, is engineering knowledge. This is based on the application of accepted scientific procedures from engineering as a region of knowledge and the scientific disciplines to which the particular area of engineering in question most clearly relates. In contrast, the management elements of the programmes are about the acquisition of skills, the reproduction of knowledge and the application of skills and knowledge in workplace contexts. This fits with the place of the MBA in management education and is clearly differentiated from the orientation of the DBA programmes studied. The industrial partnership is clearly important here in providing an integrative context, and providing participants with guidance from mentors and workplace supervisors who have a clear interest in bringing together and applying these areas of knowledge in practice.

Whilst industrial partnership is central to all the EngD programmes studied, they differ with respect to the part played by industrial partners in the delivery of the programme. In one programme the industrial mentor works closely with the research engineer to identify which courses they take. This is based on the development of competences required both by the company and the individual engineer. Here a lead is being taken by the industrial partner in determining the content of an individual's pedagogic experience. They are also involved in the delivery of aspects of the programme and in the assessment of work. In terms of the control of content, there appears to be a high degree of consensus between the academic and industrial sides of the partnership, though clearly there is recognition of differences of interest. As one course leader stated, the industrial partners wanted engineering problems solved, but had little regard beyond economic concerns for how this was achieved. In contrast, his major interest was more generally to produce 'excellent research engineers'. The research engineers themselves also wanted to look beyond the immediate context of their project to possible development and application of their research in other settings and potential for their own career development.

The breadth of content in the DBA and EdD courses is much narrower than in the EngD. Though both forms of programme could be considered to be inter-disciplinary in that they draw on a range of disciplines, for example psychology and sociology, as we indicated in the previous chapter, these discourses are recontextualized in their application to and reproduction in the fields of education and management. Neither of the two programme areas exhibits the same degree of collaboration between different regions of knowledge and practice, nor do they involve professional partners in the regulation or teaching of the content to the same extent. In these programmes, it is rather the participant who provides the interface with the professional field through reflection on and scrutiny of their everyday professional practice.

The content of the EdD and DBA courses is split between research methods/methodology and substantive content. The balance between content varies. In one DBA course, the focus of the group sessions is predominantly on research methodology and theory. Two have an equal division between research methodology and methods modules and substantive content modules. In the fourth programme, participants join a theme group and attend seminars and workshops relating to this theme, in addition to participating in generic research training workshops. The content of the programmes is guided not by an overarching assessment of the skills and competences required for advanced practitioners in the field of management, but by the evaluation of the skills and knowledge required by the individual, with a strong emphasis on research skills and the relationship of these to consultancy and other aspects of advanced practice in business and management. The emphasis on knowledge production and the relationship of this to personal practice leads to greater latitude and flexibility in terms of the content of courses. There appears not to be an accepted and stable canon of expected programme content.

The division of content of the EdD course is broadly similar. The three programmes with face-to-face taught modules have between 45 and 60 hours of group contact time per year in the taught part of the programme, with an equal split between research methods/methodology and substantive content. The substantive content here tends to relate more to consideration of contemporary issues, research and practice, than to the building of professional competence. Of the three programme areas studied, it is the EdD courses that have the least direct relationship to practice. Little explicit attention is paid to identification of competences, either relating to the profession as a whole as in the EngD or to the individual participant as in the DBA. Consequently, the relationship between course content and practice is ambiguous, uncertain or implicit. Whilst some of the modules might address research into areas of practice, the competence of the participant as a practitioner is not at issue. The relationship between professional practice and the substantive content is either rendered as a textual relation (in which links between workplace practice and the content of module are objectified in essays and other formal writing relating to the programme) or subject to personal reflection and informal discussion. The value of this should not be neglected, however. As already noted, participants and graduates from EdD programmes clearly valued the discussion with fellow participants and personal reflection on practice.

Pedagogy

Until recently, learning and teaching in Higher Education has received relatively little attention from academics and researchers. Writing on higher education pedagogy largely focussed either on giving practical advice for lecturers ('53 Interesting Ways to . . .') or the exploration of the consequences for lecturers of current understandings of the characteristics of higher knowledge and the processes of adult learning. With growing levels of participation in higher education and the attendant increase in the diversity of the student population, lecturers have become more concerned, at the level of personal practice and professional and institutional development, with the broadening of approaches to learning and teaching. The rapid development of educational technology has also prompted higher education teachers to think more broadly and creatively about pedagogy in the light of possible new modes of engagement with students both locally and at a distance.

There is also an economic dimension to this increase in interest in pedagogy. Governments are keen to ensure that their investment in higher education shows the greatest possible return. If effective and efficient learning is to take place, it is necessary to ensure that appropriate forms of pedagogy are employed. More and more government expenditure on higher education is targeted on learning and teaching, and the evaluation of teaching has become a key element in the evaluation of the quality of an institution. In England, for example, the Higher Education Funding Council (HEFCE) has made substantial sums of money available for the implementation of institutional Learning and Teaching Strategies. At the same time, the quality of teaching in individual institutions has been subject to scrutiny by the Quality Assurance Agency, first through the Subject Review process and, latterly, through the Institutional Audit. Similar initiatives and processes are in place in other countries.

The neglect of pedagogy as an issue of serious concern has been even more pronounced at doctoral level than in other phases of higher education. The key pedagogic site has traditionally been the tutorial, in which supervisor and student engage in discussion of the research project. Recent research has begun to explore the process of supervision and the relationship between supervisor and student (see, for instance, Delamont *et al.* 2000). With an increasing taught element to doctoral programmes, research into doctoral pedagogy is becoming a priority.

In addition to the general points raised above, scrutiny of doctoral pedagogy has been prompted by other factors. For instance, doctorates have increasingly come to be seen as a means of systematic training for a research career, rather than principally of value in their own right. This has led to the identification of a range of key or generic skills that cannot necessarily be incidentally and comprehensively acquired in the process of doing research. As a result, the proportions of time in PhD programmes dedicated to formally taught components have steadily increased. In the social sciences, successive editions of the ESRC postgraduate training guidelines have defined the scope of these taught components, and have stressed the importance of assessing whether or not the prescribed skills and knowledge have been acquired. The research funding councils have also shown increasing concern about the form of support that is provided to students in the development and conduct of their research. Metcalfe *et al.* (2002: 4), in their report to the Higher Education Funding Councils of England, Scotland and Wales, consider the range of action to be taken to improve the quality of research degrees outputs, including 'increasing the quality of the student/supervisor relationship'. The increased interest in doctoral level pedagogy is thus underwritten by scrutiny and regulation of both the increasingly important taught components of research degree programmes and the progressively more visible relationship between the supervisor and student.

The focus of both the development of personal practice and institutional policy has tended to be on procedures and techniques, and how these relate to outcomes. This gives us a fairly limited technical notion of pedagogy. The approach being taken here is to view pedagogy not solely as a question of technique, but to adopt a relational conception of pedagogy (see, for example, Bernstein and Solomon 1999). This focuses our attention on better understanding how different pedagogic settings are related to each other and how the manner in which tutors and participants are positioned with respect to each other relates to who acquires what in and through the programmes studied. Rather than treat 'professional doctorates' as a homogeneous category of programmes, and pedagogy as the arbitrary selection of techniques, we will attempt to explore the relationship between pedagogy and programme area in order to understand the manner in which the relations, processes and outcomes of the three professional doctorates relate to both the academic discourses on which they draw and the domains of professional practice to which they relate. In order to do this we will make some general observations about pedagogic modes and relations across the sample, before moving on to address each programme area in more detail.

Pedagogy and professional doctorates

Thus far in this chapter we have considered the pedagogic time available in the different programmes, the structure of the programmes in providing a temporal and spatial framework for the curriculum, the forms of content of the curriculum, and the relations between contents. A number of differences between the programmes have become clear. In this chapter, and in the previous chapter, we have seen that far from a homogenous group of programmes with a shared set of key attributes, there is substantial variation between the types of programmes we have studied, as well as some variation within each type. This might lead us to question the analytic utility of the classification 'professional doctorate'.

Across the programmes there were a number of explicit and tacit assumptions about the manner in which advanced, professionally relevant learning takes place. For instance, attention is paid in all programmes to the structuring of the taught components and, to varying degrees, explicit statements of the expected outcomes of pedagogic activity. Generally, clear learning outcomes were stated for each element of each programme and pacing of acquisition marked out by deadlines for submission of and feedback on assignments. Of the three programme types, the EngD courses had the most explicit and detailed outcomes (in relation to technical expertise, professional competence and managerial skills) and the tightest pacing. In one case a strict weekly pattern of taught input relating to tightly defined outcomes, related self-directed study/revision and formal testing was set up. Amongst the DBA courses, greater stress was placed upon meeting participant identified needs, for instance in one programme through the construction of a Competence Development Plan in which participants related choices to be made within the programme to their own particular professional needs. Paradoxically, least explicit attention was paid to pedagogic issues in the EdD programmes studied.

There were also clear differences between the programme types in the positioning of participants and tutors. DBA participants were presented as being senior practitioners for whom the acquisition of research expertise together with enhanced academic and practical knowledge of contemporary management would have tangible career advantages. In three of the cases, this was related to enhanced opportunities in the field of consultancy. In all cases the advantages of networking with other practitioners in the same field were also highlighted. The tutors were in most cases presented as having specific expertise in the area of research combined with specialized knowledge of particular areas of management theory or practice within a particular commercial sector. Their role in relation to the participant was framed as facilitating critical reflection on practice and guiding the development of research drawing on their expertise as supervisors and as experienced researchers.

The participants in the EdD programmes were identified as 'professionals' or 'mid-career professionals'. The value of the programmes to career development and advancement were presented in diffuse terms, for instance as providing opportunities to better understand their own professional contexts and individual practices, and to remain abreast of current educational issues. Whilst one programme claimed that many participants had gained promotion as a result of participation in the programme, the relationship between the content and process of the programme and career advancement was not clearly marked out. One key feature of the EdD programmes was that the cohort of participants was seen as providing support and opportunities for collaboration, and as acting as 'critical friends' to each other. In a similar fashion to the DBA, EdD tutors were presented as providing opportunities to reflect and 'high-quality research-led teaching'. Their ability to do this was underwritten by their experience as active researchers in the field of education and their experience supervising research students.

A key issue regarding the relationship between participants and tutors is the manner in which professional practice and academic study and research are related. The EngD is presented very much as a preparation for professional practice with enhanced career opportunities. This preparation involves specialized input from engineers from university and industrial settings and from management school staff. This in turn involves a demarcation of expertise and an academic and practical division of labour. The production of the 'research engineer', as programme participants are called, thus involves an engagement with and movement between distinct communities of practice under the guidance of expert practitioners, and requires recognition of the different interests of those communities. Participants in the DBA and EdD programmes are themselves presented as 'expert practitioners' in their own right on entry to the programme. Their tutors have research-based knowledge of a specialized field within education or business administration, expertise as a researcher and experience in the supervision of research. In the DBA programmes, engagement of tutors with professional practice is additionally through consultancy and through partnerships between business schools and specific companies. The dominant partnership, and conduit for engagement with professional practice, in both DBA and EdD programmes is, however, between tutor and participant, particularly at the thesis stage. Rather than the production of an expert identity, these programmes are involved with facilitating a transformation in identity brought about by the bringing together of the domains of research and professional practice and enabling their mutual scrutiny. Central to this is the rhetoric of critical reflection and attendant pedagogic practices. Whilst stress is placed on self-identification of needs and critical reflection on practice, there is perhaps some tension between this orientation and the ultimate examination of the outcomes of the programmes (coursework and theses) against largely, if not exclusively, academic criteria.

Pedagogic practice and relations in the EngD

All 12 of the programmes draw from a familiar range of higher education pedagogic approaches. These include lectures, workshops, seminars and tutorials. There is variation, however, in a number of respects. The EngD courses employ the greatest range of approaches. In large part, this appears to be a result of bringing together different regions of knowledge (engineering and management), different levels of study (masters level work in management and original research in engineering), different pedagogic sites (the university and the workplace) and different pedagogic agents (the university tutor and the industrial mentor). Within a particular programme approaches can range from lectures and highly structured teaching activities with unseen tests to assess acquisition; to group problem solving and simulations; to participant presentations based on reflection on workplace experiences. The highly segmented and strongly insulated nature of the university-based parts of the programme makes it possible for these different pedagogic cultures to exist alongside each other. This does, however, require the participants to resolve tensions between these approaches as they move between the different phases, segments and settings of the programme. This is particularly notable in the negotiation of differences of approach, interests and expertise between the engineering and management aspect of the programme and between the university and industrial settings. These comments from two EngD participants relate to tensions between the university and the industrial setting:

> I'd say my industrial manager is more, like, people related, then he's in a position to assess me, you know, and help whereas I'd say my academic [supervisor], well I'd say he does give advice and help on these issues, he does, he's always got that goal in mind, of, you know what it takes to get an EngD, and then you know just brings it back in line every now and again, and just makes sure you're actually doing it.

> I have a particularly academic supervisor. He's very heavily into theory, and doesn't believe in any commercial aspects of anything. So I do get some conflict, because the company want me and they want me to ask questions of commercial importance which is understandable, and that's all part of my EngD, but my academic supervisor sometimes gets upset about that, if I'm supposed to be in the university testing.

Participants become adept at handling these tensions. One refers to the process of resolution as 'an education on both sides'. Another states that:

> I will sit down and say 'Right these are the issues, let's resolve them'. And when they sit down across the table, I mean they're all nice people, they don't start shouting at each other, and then the situation gets resolved.

The approach to pedagogy in the EngD could be characterized as instrumental in that once the desired competences for research engineers are identified and the structure and content of the programme developed in relation to these, pedagogic decisions can be made on the basis of 'fitness for purpose'. These programmes require both the acquisition of tightly specified skills and knowledge and the development of the ability to make multifaceted professional decisions in complex workplace settings. A complex of pedagogical approaches, rather than development of a unified and coherent pedagogic orientation is instrumentally adopted in order to facilitate the acquisition of this diverse range of skills and knowledge.

A heterogeneous approach like this is also made tenable by the positioning of participants as trainees. As we have already seen, the EngD for the most part aims to take the best recent graduates and, through a challenging and multi-faceted programme, prepare them for rapid promotion in industrial management. The programmes are thus engaged in the production of identities, achieved in collaboration between academic and industrial partners. The research engineer is 'produced' in this process, and academic and industrial practices, and relations between them, are reproduced. In contrast, in the DBA and EdD, it is the participants themselves, as experienced practitioners, who provide the link between the university and diverse workplace settings. For the most part, these settings, in all but general terms, are unknown to the university staff. There is not the same form of partnership in the production of professional identities in these programmes.

It is interesting to note that the EngD programme that is most active in attracting participants who are experienced, and sometimes senior, practitioners has developed portfolio-based assessment and utilizes project work in the assessment of taught components, which moves some way towards integrating the diverse range of skills, knowledge and experience, whilst still allowing these to be assessed in a variety of ways. It is also notable in this programme that it is the industrial mentor who advises on and has responsibility for the overall development and progress through the programme of the research engineer. In providing advice on the participant's research project, the academic and industrial mentors work together. The academic mentor has specific responsibility for ensuring that the project meets accepted academic standards and for providing feedback to the participant on this.

Whilst the other EngD programmes do not give such extensive responsibility to the industrial mentor, a similar division of labour is implemented with respect to the research project. The university tutors positioned themselves as experts in their particular field of knowledge with responsibility for ensuring that academic criteria were met and high standards maintained. In all cases, the project was supervised by a team or partnership containing both academics and industrialists and a clear division of responsibilities was stated. In each case, the pedagogic relation is such that the participant is positioned as subordinate to the academic tutor and industrial mentor with respect to both academic and the workplace settings and discourses. One participant refers to the experience as 'like an apprenticeship'. Another mentions 'getting drafts back from your supervisor that have got red scribble all over them'. A number of students make reference to the 'specialist knowledge' or 'tremendous experience' of their academic supervisor and industrial mentor. As one participant observes of his mentor:

> He has such a vast knowledge of the field he's in. Because I'm only new to it I could, like, had he been [in] every day, and I would quite easily be a sponge and just sponge in the information that he knows, his knowledge.

Pedagogic practice and relations in the DBA

The DBA programmes have a very different pedagogic orientation. Whereas the EngD employs a range of approaches, including highly didactic forms of pedagogy, the DBA courses were explicitly participant-centred in approach. Participants were clearly positioned as having responsibility for their own learning. In one case this was managed through reflection on individual competence development plans. It was explicitly stated that learning was 'self-directed' and that the development of competences extended well beyond the programme. The university aimed to work with participants to develop a 'culture of scholarship'. In another of the programmes it was stated that participants should be engaging in a 'developmental, reflective and creative learning process which is linked to the essential outcomes of the programme'. Tutors attempted to avoid the didactic presentation of knowledge and information by requiring participants to engage extensively with first order and primary sources. Tutor led sessions focus on analysis of these materials rather than exposition. Through both individual and group work, efforts are made to challenge established positions, methods and methodologies. The use of critical reviews and participant presentations support this. All the DBA courses adopt similar forms of workshop-based pedagogy, combined with individual and group supervision and other group-based work establishing dialogue between participants and tutors.

In all the DBA programmes, the participant is seen as being a senior practitioner with distinct and well-developed expertise in the field of professional practice. One programme identifies the participants as management consultants, senior managers from the public and private sectors and business school academics. They are viewed as being mature and with an international perspective. The programme is presented as adding to or enhancing existing advanced knowledge and expertise. It is for people 'who wish to enhance, modify or change their careers by advanced management research, underpinned by substantial theory and adding to their personal, research and consultancy competences'. The other programmes mirrored this, mentioning technical facility with research, the development and use of advanced research skills, the ability to understand and manage complex issues and to relate theory, research and practice. They also stress the development of personal, organizational, communication and professional skills. They claim that participants are gaining unique insight into their professional practice and becoming part of a 'community of research practitioners' and member of a range of professional networks. Though there is a strong emphasis on professional context and practice, the programmes rarely engage directly with these contexts or agents within them. The participant provides the link between the university and the workplace. The individual focus, for instance in the identification of competences, and the stress placed on building consultancy skills leads to a marginalization of the specific organizational setting within which the participant is working. The emphasis is very much on development of the individual in relation to professional practice, not on the development of a particular organization through research. This is evident in the interviews with participants and graduates, who stressed the part that the doctorate had played in the development of their own personal professional skills.

With the stress placed on individual responsibility for learning and the existing advanced professional skills of the participants, the university tutors are positioned as supporting the development of the research by providing expert help and guidance. Their expertise, in both their own accounts and those of the participants, is as experienced researchers and supervisors, some with an international reputation in their specialist field. In interviews, participants stated that they did not expect their supervisor to be an expert practitioner in their particular professional field. From working with their university supervisor, they want clear expert advice on the development of their research and to gain insight and expertise in the processes of research. The networking and contact with other professionals in and through the programme is also highly valued.

In the case of the DBA, it appears that, in relation to professional practice, discourses and settings, the participant is not subordinate to the university tutor. The expertise of the tutor is clearly in the area of research. The expectation is that they will provide guidance and create the environment for the development of research and the building of research competence, and through this supplement the professional expertise of the participant.

The university, however, retains control of the regulative and evaluative criteria for what counts as legitimate research, and the ultimate outcome of the programme is dependent on this. Though the development of broader competences and professional practice are highlighted in the programmes, ultimate responsibility for this rests with the individual participant. This is monitored by the tutor but is not the object of direct pedagogic action, regulation or evaluation. A spread of expertise is offered in the supervision of research in all cases through the use of a supervisory team. In one case, this can include a workplace-based supervisor if appropriate. All programmes place great importance on sharing the research process and outcomes with fellow participants and peers, and the publication of research in either professional or academic journals.

Pedagogic practice and relations in the EdD

The EdD programmes exhibit a higher degree of ambiguity with respect to pedagogy and pedagogic relations. These programmes share an emphasis on the production of new knowledge through research, and the use of the taught part of the programme to develop the required skills and knowledge. Group work is used, and the production of a supportive research environment is stressed in each case. Alongside this, emphasis is also placed on structured teaching to build research skills. The literature on one of the programmes states that it seeks 'to provide a supportive, structured and effective learning environment in which experienced professionals in education and related fields are enabled to explore professional concerns within a critical framework, and to undertake original, high-quality independent research'. Likewise, another programme states that it provides 'the opportunity to reflect on educational issues through . . . structured, professional teaching and study informed by the most up-to-date research and, where relevant, inspection findings'.

Pedagogically, the EdD programmes lie between the EngD and the DBA programmes. They do not employ the heterogeneous approach of EngD, nor do they have the clearly defined self-directed learning ideology of the DBA programmes. Similarly, they do not attempt to identify the key professional competences required either from a professional and academic standpoint, as the EngD, or from the perspective of the individual practitioner, as the DBA. Participants are seen as mid-career professionals who want, according to one programme, 'to achieve a doctorate, both to enhance their current performance and as an investment in their future careers. Many participants have received promotion as a result of their participation in the programme.' Another states that participants are 'professionals in education and related disciplines who wish to keep abreast of a range of educational topics and refine their research skills'. The acquisition of research skills together with the greater understanding of ones own practice that results from conducting workplace-focussed research are seen as being of value in their own right. The skills developed are not presented as being directly relevant to professional practice, but rather helping the individual reflect on and illuminate their own practice and practice within the institutions they are working in. Whilst the participants and graduates were clear about the value the EdD had for the development of their practice, and in some cases had tangible benefits for their career, this was qualitatively different from the more direct relevance, in different ways, of the EngD and DBA.

Tutors are positioned as specialists in a field of education, but not necessarily expert practitioners. It is expertise in research, experience as an active researcher, and specialist knowledge in the area being studied that are expected. Supervision does not as a principle, in any of the cases studied, involve practitioners, but can be joint with another academic. One area of professional relevance that does mark out the EdD is that both tutor and participant are involved in education and therefore share a professional interest in, for instance, learning, teaching and assessment. In addition they have common knowledge and experience of contemporary policies, conditions and relations in education. Given this, it is puzzling that, in terms of curriculum, pedagogy and assessment, the EdD programmes are the most conservative of the programmes studied.

Conclusion

By focusing on the structure of the programmes, the curriculum content and pedagogic modes, practices and relations, we have been able to explore differences between the three programme areas studied and to begin to relate these differences to specific features of the academic discourses on which the programmes draw and the relationship between these and professional practice. From our discussion we might conclude that, whilst the label 'professional doctorate' has helped open up a space for the development of new forms of programme that in turn bring new participants into doctoral level education, as a descriptive and analytic category it now has limited utility. From the consideration of the case-study programmes, we have seen that practices, processes, outcomes and relations between academic discourses and professional practice and between academic tutors and professional practitioners vary greatly between programme areas. It has also become clear that, certainly in the cases studied here, practice does not appear to live up to expectations, in terms of curriculum, pedagogy and assessment, of those who celebrate the transformative potential of professional doctorates. Despite their many points of departure from the conventional PhD, the professional doctorates appear to continue to reproduce existing forms of academic and professional practice and reinforce established relations between academic and professional discourses.

We have, however, been able to reach a better understanding of how the variation within and between the three programme relates to a variety of factors, including the relationship between each of the regions of knowledge (business/management, education and engineering), disciplined knowledge and professional practice. With respect to these relationships, there appear to be different 'levels of confidence' within each area studied, which in turn establish a different form of relation between the professional doctorate, academic knowledge and professional practice. In engineering, for instance, there is a high level of confidence in both the relationship between engineering knowledge and scientific disciplines, such as physics, and between scholarship and research in engineering and the quality of professional practice. Whilst academic and professional practice are clearly shaped and regulated by different interests and imperatives, there appears to be a strong mutually recognized interrelationship between the two. This provides the basis for a strong state-sponsored instrumental initiative for the production of research engineers through doctoral programmes that are internally and externally highly regulated. In management and education, the level of confidence between foundation disciplines and these particular regions of knowledge are less secure, as is the relationship between academic knowledge and research in these areas and professional practice in business and education. Consequently, the benefits of participation in a professional doctorate programme in these fields are located at the level of the individual. This is particularly the case with business administration, where the emphasis is placed on the development of consultancy skills and the personal identification of competences to be developed. The predominantly institutional location of educational practice makes the position and orientation of the EdD more ambiguous. Participation in the programme and production of research are clearly of benefit to participants, and often indirectly to their institutions. There are no clearly defined competences, nor strong direct links with professional settings. Scepticism about the value of research for the development of educational practice (see, for instance, Tooley and Darby 1998) further contributes to the ambiguity of the nature of the individual benefits of the EdD and the wider development of professional and institutional practice.

Looking at each programme area in turn, we can see something of the distinctive characteristics of these relationships. The DBA programmes build on the participants' localized personal assessments of professional competence. Business, as a competitive field of practice, can be seen as having a pragmatic orientation, with a concern for what works, or rather what is seen to work, and what gives a competitive advantage. Whilst knowledge production is important, a pragmatic orientation can destabilize knowledge creation and lead to a succession of trends and shifts in relation to economic and commercial conditions. Currently, with a perceived shift to a knowledge- rather than production-based economy, at least in the most developed economies, knowledge production and research are seen as valuable professional skills. The personal skills orientation of the MBA is carried over into the DBA, which focuses on the production rather than reproduction of knowledge, but through the development of critical and research skills that are more widely applicable, notably in consultancy work. Close attention is paid to the field of practice but there is no assessment of quality of individual practice by the university. This assessment is made reflectively by the practitioner, as are any links that might be made with institutional development. As is clear from both the marketing of DBA courses and the comments of participant and graduates, doing a DBA is very much a personal professional investment.

In engineering, the programmes are driven by professionally and academically identified competences that are well defined and clearly recognizable. There is a partnership between the university and the profession to regulate these and to induct, monitor and assess practitioners. The pedagogic approach is instrumental, allowing a broad range of forms of pedagogy and assessment, and supported by high levels of confidence in the relationship between engineering and both professional and disciplined academic knowledge. This instrumental approach also allows successful collaboration with other regions of knowledge, in this case management and business administration. The development of the skills and knowledge of the individual research engineer through the EngD programme is seen as making a contribution at a variety of levels: the individual's career development and advancement, the development of the profession through the creation of new generations of skilled engineering managers, the solution of specific engineering-related problems in partner institutions, the contribution to more general applied knowledge in engineering and the development of the regional and national (production based) economy.

In education, individual personal and intellectual development comes to the fore. Although claims are made for a close relationship between the EdD programme and personal professional and institutional development, this is indirect and achieved through personal reflection, the production of new knowledge through personal research and the benefits to peers and institutions of the institutionally located process of the scrutiny of practice and the conduct of research. The quality of the research and other writing is monitored, regulated and evaluated by the university. Professional practice and development is addressed and discussed, in dialogue with tutors and peers, but is not directly evaluated within the programmes. There appears to be a focus on textual production (that is essays and theses), through which professional practice is objectified. This is underpinned by a seemingly insecure relationship between education as a region of knowledge and both professional practice and academic disciplines. This results in conservative pedagogy and assessment. Related to this, concern is expressed by tutors about the perceived relationship to the PhD in education and comparative status of the EdD. There is also an unclear relationship with masters level qualifications in education, some of which provide an induction into research in education and others of which have a distinctly professional orientation. This ambiguity is further compounded by the growth of a parallel pathway of professional qualifications, for example the National Professional Qualification for Headteachers (NPQH). As yet, the relationship between existing academic qualifications in education, emerging professional qualifications and professionally oriented research programmes such as the EdD is unclear.

In the next section of the book we examine the reasons students give for undertaking professional doctorate study, and the trajectories of those students on the three programmes, as they progress through their chosen forms of study.

Part 4

Trajectories

8
Motivation

Introduction

Two of the characteristics of the professional doctorate, frequently used to distinguish it from the PhD, are its mission to contribute to practice and its orientation towards established professionals. Bourner *et al.* (2001b: 70) suggest, for example, that professional doctorates 'address the career needs of practising professionals, particularly those in, or who aspire to, senior positions within their profession'. Hall (1996: 162) identifies those who join an EdD programme as 'mid-career professional educators' and 'competent learners'; and Gregory (1997: 19) reinforces this by pointing out that the EdD 'is aimed at practitioners or educational leaders'. Bareham and Bourner (2000) further suggest that it is senior managers who undertake the DBA, while Evans (1997: 177) reminds us that the distinctiveness of these programmes lies in the 'richness of students' professional contexts and their position of having to balance senior work responsibilities and family commitments with their research'. This implies a distinct population from that of the PhD; and this is supported by Humphrey and McCarthy (1999), who acknowledge the varied nature of postgraduate learners, while Pearson (1999) outlines the growing diversity of doctoral learners generally. However, discussion specifically on professional doctorates has tended to regard these programmes and learners on them as homogenous and contrast them with those undertaking a PhD (Lee *et al.* 2000), but while the rapid growth of programmes such as the EdD, DBA and EngD continue (Bourner *et al.* 2000a), little evidence exists about the profiles of learners, and more particularly their motivation for undertaking these doctorates. This chapter therefore looks at learner aspirations and motivations for undertaking professional doctorates, and seeks to show that in practice professional doctorate students are extremely varied and present complex sets of expectations that differ both across and within programme types.

Debates concerning learner motivation in general are complex (Breen and Lindsay 1999). However, the concepts of intrinsic and extrinsic motivation that are frequently used are helpful in this context, and we draw on these in the analysis that follows. Extrinsic motivation is governed by the goals, values and interests of others as they affect the individual, and participation in an activity is driven primarily by the prospect of external, tangible reward. Pintrich and Schunk (1996: 33) define extrinsic motivation as 'motivation to engage in an activity as a means to an end. Individuals who are extrinsically motivated work on tasks because they believe that participation will result in desirable outcomes such as a reward, teacher praise, or avoidance of punishment'. Breen and Lindsay (1999: 78) support this by describing extrinsic motivation as the 'process of satisfying a need which is related to the learning activity, but is not satisfied by the learning itself'. Intrinsic motivation on the other hand is defined by Pintrich and Schunk (1996: 33) as the engagement in an activity '. . . for its own sake. People who are intrinsically motivated work on tasks because they find them enjoyable.' Naccaroto (1988) describes it as the pursuit of a task for its inherent pleasure and as a result, the learner is less likely to be driven by an incentive or reward other than an innate interest in the subject material itself.

In this chapter, our prime concern is with the initial reasons for undertaking a professional doctorate, and we suggest that students on different types of programmes have different motivations for joining them. The greatest distinction is between the EngD and the DBA/EdD programmes, with DBA and EdD learners displaying a similarity in both their profiles and motivations. Three models of motivation are presented as characterizing professional doctorate students; however, these constructs in practice are unlikely to exist in isolation and elements of all three could conceivably feature to varying degrees within an individual student. Nevertheless, the creation of a loose typology provides a helpful means of clarifying the different motivational forms, their varying features and their interrelationships. We have therefore identified three distinct types: Type 1: extrinsic-professional initiation; Type 2: extrinsic-professional continuation; and Type 3: instrinsic-personal/professional affirmation.

Type 1: Extrinsic-professional initiation

In Types 1 and 2 the value of knowledge and the motivation for acquiring it lie in the external rewards that the learner believes will result (in this case career enhancement). Type 1 motivation (extrinsic-professional initiation) is consequently characterized by the learner who identifies their doctorate directly with career development. Typically the learner will be in the early stages of their career with some, albeit limited, professional experience. For this student, the professional doctorate presents four key attractions: accelerated promotion; management training; acquisition of experience; and financial support.

Accelerated promotion

For the learner driven by Type 1 motivation, career enhancement and preparation for a career in industry are important. Here, an EngD graduate reflects on why he embarked on the doctorate and the value that the doctorate's link with industry offered:

> I was quite aware at the time that if I chose to do a straight PhD that people with straight PhD qualifications tend to be regarded as a bit academic or a bit distant from the real world; and the Barnaby Report was really saying that the EngD should be set up to try to tackle that preconception, and that fitted exactly with my views and interest. I'm interested in research. I've always done jobs that involve some sort of research or development or something, even if they're not labelled as research jobs; but I'm also interested in the practical aspect of that, of the applied aspect of it, and I thought with the EngD I would have a broader choice of the kind of roles that I could go into afterwards. I thought I could still stay in academic roles if I wanted to and in that area I would be able to contribute more to the running of the institution. Likewise, if I wanted to go into industry or consultancy, that it should give me a slightly sharper sword as it were in that respect. I suppose it was about not trying to shut doors really, or trying to open more doors, rather than close them.

For some learners the doctorate not only represents a means of gaining some form of employment, but also provides the opportunity in the long-term of holding a position of seniority within their anticipated professional area. Another EngD learner characterized his EngD programme as a means of extending his promotion opportunities:

> I wanted to continue my education because of the job I got at the time. I realised that I wasn't going to get much further without getting some more qualifications, and the EngD seemed the best way to be able to prove myself and get the recognition I wanted.

The immersion of the learner within an industrial or workplace setting is an important factor in enabling this professional acceleration. This type of learner is unlikely to be employed as an engineer at the start of the doctorate and therefore requires the doctorate to provide a route into their profession. The learner comes with the expectation that the doctorate will provide them with a good job, possibly within the organization that has been their research site.

Management training

Students motivated by professional initiation perceive the opportunity for management training as valuable and regard it as an integral part of enabling them to begin work at a more senior level and to obtain promotion. The three EngD students below suggest that management training is an important part of being inducted into industry, and this sets it apart from the PhD:

> I started doing an EngD because it's perceived to offer something extra like management training stuff, and as part of my degree I'd taken a year out and did some PhD research, and afterwards I did the Masters as well, and you sort of think to yourself on the research side, 'I'm really interested in that', but if you're going to go out into industry or whatever, you're going to hit the ground and then fall on your face because you are not going to be in tune with industrial practice or anything like that. Whereas with this, you know that you've got an outlet, working with cars. You get into a sort of management mindset; you get to know how to think; you get to know how a business runs from the inside.

> And I did an EngDoc because I wanted to do research but I didn't want to be based in a laboratory all the time, and an EngDoc allows you to get into your workplace and just experience what's going on in the workplace. And I like research but I'm more interested in the broader aspects of the management side of it, the interpersonal skills, that sort of thing, and I thought that was a good way to blend a higher qualification which you've got to have because so many people have first degrees now, and also get experience in industry as well.

> The EngD guaranteed me four years of integrated training professionally and research whereas with the EngRes I didn't have any guarantee that I was going to be able to carry on the research project into a PhD. So it was the blend of the management with the research on the EngD. But it was because it was co-ordinated as a whole programme. I know some of the other EngD schools have got several portfolios.

These three students are making a number of points about their reasons for undertaking professional doctorate study, and not registering for a PhD. They have identified a specific workplace culture, knowledge of which constitutes an integral part of successful practice within it. This can be gained through experience in industry, but it can also be acquired by studying on a professional doctorate programme, which is perceived as combining research activity, management and training, and the development of products, which allow the industry to compete in the marketplace.

Acquisition of experience

The direct relevance of the doctorate to professional practice is the third element in this motivational type. It is not simply that the learner considers the subject matter transferable to the workplace, but it is also the opportunity to acquire professional experience whilst doing research that is regarded as critical in ultimately gaining employment in the profession. A final-year EngD student suggests that:

> I did a sandwich course at university so I'd spent a year working in industry before I'd finished my bachelors degree, and when I'd finished I wanted to get a doctorate qualification, but I didn't want to leave the industry particularly being a female and working in a heavy engineering firm. This [the EngD] gave me the opportunity to continue my professional development. I've now got my chartered engineer status, and get a doctorate qualification at the same time. And that's basically why I did it, because I didn't want to take three years out to do a PhD, and not have any working experience with it.

Gaining a doctorate as part of one's professional experience is not therefore seen as taking time out of work but rather integrating professional training with the acquisition of a professionally relevant qualification. An EngD student who clearly valued the orientation towards practice and professional relevance echoed this. It also provided him with the opportunity of acquiring professional experience as well as a doctoral qualification, which he considered to be an advantage of the EngD over the PhD:

> Personally, I quite liked the idea of doing some postgraduate study, but what put me off a PhD was the fact that it's primarily theoretical, whereas the EngD has got a much more practical basis. There's a definite end result, which you can use in practice.

Another EngD student expressed a similar view:

> I wanted to do research but I didn't want to be based in a laboratory all the time, and an EngDoc allows you to get into your workplace and just experience what is going on. I like research but I'm more interested in the broader aspects of the management side of it, the interpersonal skills, that sort of thing; and I thought that was a good way to blend a higher qualification which you've got to have, because so many people have the first degrees now and get also experience in industry as well.

What is interesting about the views expressed here is that the qualification has currency in its own right, and in addition, the programme allows participants to gain valuable experience in industry, which is essential for coping with the many demands such a career will make on the student.

Financial support

Financial support is the final element of the Type 1 construct. This featured prominently in the motivation of EngD students in particular and reflects the profile of the Type 1 learner whose young age and limited professional experience means that it is less likely that they will have personal financial assets to draw upon and may make them more dependent upon external support. Because of the functional nature of their goals, it follows that the Type 1 learner is also concerned with the functionality and viability of the research process. It is also likely that the higher student bursary awarded to EngDs by the EPSRC is an important factor for the Type 1 student in tipping the balance between choosing to study an EngD rather than a PhD, as one EngD student alludes to below:

> I'm not ashamed to say it, because it paid well. I didn't want to do a traditional PhD and suffer another three years of near poverty.

Type 1 is particularly representative of the EngD learner profile which is likely to be a result of these programmes' aims to develop future leaders in the field, as a preparation for becoming 'managers of research . . . innovators of the future' (Evans 1997: 1). Nevertheless, the association of this degree with career-related outcomes does mean that the Type 1 learner brings to the programme a high expectation of what the doctorate will ultimately deliver. This kind of motivation for research reflects Brew's model of investment (2001: 125) where research is associated with a strong economic or technical rationality and a need to demonstrate industrial relevance. Engagement with research in Brew's model is particularly focussed on outcomes and implies commitment to the research process in order to accomplish higher professional goals.

As well as this professional initiation type motivation being reflected in EngD learners, Smith (2002) found similar characteristics in his study of American EdDs. He found that learners exhibited two distinct cultures, and of interest here is the 'vocational culture' where emphasis is given by students to training and skill development in order to function effectively (in this instance in educational administration, the focus of this particular EdD). This evidence and the extracts above present a model of motivation where the learner identifies a strong correlation between the doctorate, a perceived set of capabilities and enhanced career development opportunities, with the possibility of accelerated promotion. However, the symbolic importance and sense of status that this learner identifies with the doctorate may not necessarily be associated with the better execution of a task. The perceived link is between accomplishment of the doctorate and enhanced promotion, not necessarily enhanced performance. Hesketh and Knight (1999: 152) discuss credentialism and the relationship between education and 'a better chance of getting a job of choice' as increasingly synonymous with motivation for higher education. However, what is clear in this Type 1 model is that motivation for professional initiation is related to both the learners' age and level of experience (that is, relatively young and inexperienced), neither of which feature in Hesketh and Knight's analysis.

Type 2: Extrinsic-professional continuation

Type 2 motivation shares the extrinsic notions of external rewards and achievements as direct consequences of engaging in a particular activity, but in contrast to the Type 1 learner, the Type 2 learner will be reasonably established in their professional field and have some professional experience. Motivation for the doctorate is principally governed by further developing their professional career either in line with existing work, or by providing new opportunities for diversifying career options. This model has three key characteristics; career development; contribution to practice; and programme structure.

Career development

Career development or developing ways for expanding one's career opportunities are important motives for the learner with Type 2 motivation. One EdD student who was extremely interested in the process of research made the following comment:

> I am seriously thinking now that it would be a career move that I'd like to do. It's not likely to be a profitable career move. It would only be a sideways move, taking up some underpaid research job; but you know, it is opening up the idea of developing that side rather than just developing the administrative side of the job.

Another EdD student said about their programme that:

> I also felt that it would help me in the long run in terms of my career, which subsequently proved to be true, because I left that job at the end of last year and became Director of Education for another distance learning institution. And that was certainly part of me getting that job.

What motivates these students is not just moving up the career ladder in their particular workplaces, but also seeking new opportunities within the professional matrix of which they are a part.

Contributing to practice

Type 2 motivation is underpinned by Boud and Garrick's (1999) notion of learning as a social investment, where the pursuit of research is largely focussed on making a contribution to the learners' own immediate organizational context or more broadly to their professional field. Learners with this motivation are concerned that the doctorate provides opportunities for them to give something back to the organizational context in which they work. Breadth of perspective is also regarded as important, and learners in this category want to acquire a better understanding of their business to affect its long-term development.

Contributing to or improving the way in which professional practice is conducted is also a valuable incentive for learners in this category. Seeking knowledge that can be directly applied in practice, or finding a way of examining a problem or improving practice is central for these learners; and for those in a mid career position, the doctorate can offer a means of enhancing their competitive edge in their professional field.

Programme structure

The particularly structured nature of professional doctorates is important for the learner in this motivational category. Wlodkowski (1985) argues that a key aspect of adult learning is that the learner is highly pragmatic in their motivation, whilst Hall (1996: 163) discusses the importance of a structured approach to doctoral study and describes the process of an EdD as being 'mapped out as a series of small steps . . . rather than one big mammoth journey'. An EdD student supports this in the following way:

> I chose the EdD basically because I was attracted by the way it was split into two parts and the first part producing the six assignments. I thought that was a much more supportive environment, and I don't think I had the confidence in my own ability to go on to a PhD which I see as a rather isolated experience.

Another EdD student felt that the structure was important in providing discipline and momentum:

> I didn't feel I could do a PhD because my own job was quite demanding, and my home life was quite demanding, and I felt that I needed a structure whereby I had a sort of timetable where I had to submit work by certain times, and that would give me the structure that would get me through the time sort of phase of it. It would give a certain amount of discipline to me that I might not have if I was doing a PhD. I've got colleagues who have done PhDs, or either who have tried PhDs, and I thought I wanted to try and give myself the best chance.

At times, students displayed a lack of self-confidence and a lack of belief in their ability to complete the programme, and they certainly perceived a more structured approach as a means of completing their doctoral study. This issue of confidence reflects Entwistle and Ramsden's (1983: 6) notion of a fear of failure, where they describe the student as not possessing enough 'self confidence and anxiously aware of assessment requirements'. The structured approach to study presented by these professional doctorates offers students repeated and immediate rewards to sustain their motivation; and implies a greater dependency relationship between learners and teachers, and a need for closer guidance than might be the case with a PhD learner.

Type 3: Intrinsic-personal/professional affirmation

In contrast to Types 1 and 2 where the learner is motivated primarily by the instrumental use of a doctorate for the external reward of employment or career development, Type 3 is characterized by intrinsic motivation and is governed by those goals, interests and values held by the individual. Here, the learner is concerned with self-determination (Deci and Ryan 1985), and the intention to pursue the doctorate for its own sake. For learners motivated by Type 3, their professional career is more likely to already be established when they begin a doctorate, and therefore the age and professional experience of the learner is greater than for those that are motivated by our first type. This experience may be extremely varied in nature and may have culminated in the learner occupying a senior position by the time they begin the doctorate. The following profile provided by a DBA tutor illustrates the extensive experience and seniority that one of his students possessed:

> His career has evolved from financial management via consultancy to general management, and he has served at Board and senior management level in a number of public and private companies. Industry experience has been gained in power and water engineering, shipbuilding, printing and publishing, oil exploration and production, specialist building products and automotive services. Much of the last fifteen years has been spent helping the shareholders and managements of emerging, growth and middle market companies – especially privately held companies – to evaluate and finance growth opportunities, release liquidity for shareholders, and bring about changes in performance.

The Type 3 learner may reflect intrinsic factors that could broadly be described as cognitive (a keenness to maintain attention to something interesting, to develop meaning or understanding or to solve a problem); while others are more affective and will be concerned with increasing their feelings of well-being, or enhancing a sense of self-esteem. Consequently, two key factors characterize Type 3: personal fulfilment and professional credibility.

Personal fulfilment

Here, the doctorate is closely associated with a sense of accomplishment and the reflections below from an EdD graduate highlight this:

> Well, I've been a teacher all my professional life. I logged 40 years in the profession. Traditional background, English degree at university, London Royal Holloway College, Cambridge Institute of Education PGCE, into grammar schools, secondary technical school, secondary

modern and then followed my husband into comprehensive education. So we went into comprehensive teaching in Harlow in the 1960s, and then I had children. I was a traditional mother who left when the first baby was on the way. But just before I left I was the Head of Department, Head of English in a large comprehensive school in Essex, 1,500 pupils. I dropped out to have a baby because the nursery facilities were non-existent unless you were a single mother or had a disabled child. We lived nowhere near our mothers-in-law so I became a housewife and subsequently had two more children. My husband raced up the career tree and eventually became a headmaster, so I did part-time work. Fortunately I did things like evening school. I was always interested in education because I come from an educational background. My father was the Principal of a Further Education College in Lancashire and had been a tutor at Bolton Technical Teachers Training Institute, and I was always involved in education. So when my children were going through school, I was always interested. The crunch sort of came when I tried to get back into teaching, when the children, I felt were old enough to manage. I'd done evening classes at the FE College and then I went back into full-time teaching. And I had to go in at the bottom line – Head of Department has to go in as an ordinary English teacher, and I had the double disadvantage of having dropped out and of being married to one of the local head teachers. And it was a hard struggle. I never felt that I missed out on seniority because, in a sense, I shared senior management excitement by being married to a head-teacher. Then our eldest son took a Masters degree. As he finished, I said 'you know, I'd really like to do that'. And the children said 'well, why not?', and advertised in the magazine of ATL was the Master of Education. So I wrote off for that, and joined the course in 1993 and it ran to the end. It was a three-year course but, at the end of two years, we were told it was changing its name and also they were starting a doctorate course. And out of the 15 or so of us, half a dozen said, 'what about getting on the doctorate course?', and they said to these half a dozen of us, 'we think you can do it. We're prepared to let you take your credits into the doctorate programme', and I remember listening to this and thinking, 'oh that's nice, they're willing to take me on a doctoral programme. I can't do it.' And I went home and said to my husband: 'guess what? They've suggested that I and half a dozen others could join the doctoral programme. But I don't think I'll bother'. And he said: 'don't be stupid. Go for it'. And I rang the children up and they all said 'go for it, mother'.

This learner evidently didn't expect the doctorate to make a significant difference to her professional profile and in fact appears to have embarked on it for the intellectual challenge. The support of this learner's family has played an important part in her believing that she has the ability to undertake a programme at this level.

Professional credibility

Particularly for those learners with substantial professional experience the doctorate provides a means of externally validating knowledge and expertise that was perhaps considered to be previously unacknowledged. This was the case for one DBA student who was attracted to this doctorate because he saw it as a way of getting:

> some kind of business credential that reinforces what I've done over so many years. There was more appeal in the glamour of it rather than having truthfully understood the endurance on which I was about to embark. The qualification was of comparable academic standing but practice-based, wasn't about to go off and become a researcher, but the relevance to me was to be able to research something that was more than reasonably related to practice beyond retirement.

Type 3 motivation is more likely to lead to research that is 'curiosity-driven' (Brew 2001: 124), and that is viewed as personally transformative or linked to a process of personal discovery and change. For this learner the research process or experience of engaging with a doctorate is about more than just addressing a research question in order to collect data and create results. It is about embarking on an activity that requires engagement of the self, where the research journey symbolizes much of the learners' personal as well as professional life (Brew 2001: 132).

This appears to reflect liberal notions concerning the pursuit of truth and development of critical engagement that is frequently associated with the traditional function of the university (and indeed the PhD). Hence, the Type 3 learner presents a greater concern for the research process rather than the product, and this process represents the bringing together and utilization of professional experience and expertise with personal interest. While the concern will primarily be with doing research on an individual level, it may be undertaken to achieve professional affirmation. This apparent need for some learners to gain recognition for their professional excellence from an external, validating source (in this case the university) may stem in some cases from negative past educational experiences and therefore result in a perceived need to prove their own professional and personal self-worth. In such cases the *status* of the doctorate is important, even though the title 'Dr' may not actually be professionally beneficial (and indeed in some cases may be viewed as disadvantageous). Delanty (2001: 113) suggests that new approaches to knowledge production (cf. Gibbons *et al.* 1994) neglect to address the fact that while the university may no longer be the sole producer of knowledge, it is still the 'most important dispenser of credentials and is also a significant arbiter of cultural capital, such as status'. This is certainly apparent for those learners motivated by Type 3, who are seeking external endorsement for their existing professional expertise and look to the university as a site that possesses appropriate standing.

Conclusion

These three models of motivation highlight the diversity of expectations that learners present when undertaking professional doctorates. Many of the learners displayed predominantly goal-orientated motivation linking the doctorate with different aspects of their professional career, and these models show the various ways in which learners construct relationships between the programme of study and professional enhancement.

All of these models have rewards of different kinds attached to them and different measures of achievement. For example, in the Type 1 model the measure is whether the learner ultimately finds meaningful employment on completion (an extrinsic measure), whereas gauging whether learners have gained a sense of personal fulfilment (Type 3) is far more deep-rooted and can only be measured by intrinsic means. The extent to which these motivational models can be used as predictors of performance is debatable and in any case would require learners to be tracked throughout the course of their doctorate to completion in order to systematically evaluate changes in their concept of motivation. However, as they are constructs, the distinctions between motivational types will no doubt be blurred in reality and the form of motivation presented by a student is more likely to be a question of emphasis rather than exhibiting one type in isolation. Certainly if Breen and Lindsay's (1999) argument that all motivation ultimately stems from some form of intrinsic need is to be accepted, there will inevitably be a complex interrelationship between these different factors.

This typology however, does suggest a correlation between programme type and motivational type, although clearly there are differences within the three types of doctorate as well as between. In addition, how learners comprehend the value of a professional doctorate varies. In general, the greatest distinction lies between the EngD and the DBA/EdD. EngD learners appear motivated by Type 1 factors (extrinsic-professional initiation), whereas Types 2 and 3 appear more synonymous with the DBA and EdD programmes. The issue that most differentiates the three types of motives is the relationship of the doctorate with the participant's career. For those participants with Type 1 motivation (the majority of which are EngD), the doctorate features early on in their professional life and the role that it is subsequently expected to play is that of career initiation. On the other hand, EngD participants were principally motivated to begin this type of doctorate by extrinsic factors. Many of these factors concerned career development and the acquisition of skills and experience to enhance their employability. Pragmatic factors such as financial support also featured as an important reason as to why this doctorate had been chosen over the PhD. There is a general sense of instrumentality associated with this set of motives as in many cases learners identified the EngD in connection with the success and reward of accelerated career development.

In contrast, those with Types 2 and 3 motivation are more likely to be established professionals with the doctorate intersecting their career at a much later stage. The role of the doctorate for these individuals is inclined towards some form of continuing professional development. This trend reflects Wlodkowski's (1985: 8) argument that young adults are largely concerned with education for 'upward career mobility', whereas older adults are looking for 'better job opportunities when this is possible, and those reaching career levels with few possibilities for career improvement are often interested in learning that will enhance the quality of life'.

These different relationships between doctorate and career mean that the different roles experience and expertise play also differ. For the Type 1 learner substantial professional experience has yet to be acquired. The doctorate is seen as enabling this acquisition process both on completion as a means to ultimately gaining employment, but also, during the process of the doctorate, by gaining experience in the workplace alongside the qualification. Because the professional doctorate represents career initiation and a process of acquiring experience, it also represents a process of developing expertise. Students wanted to obtain new knowledge and skills, particularly in relation to management and business. The notion of an 'integrated professional training' suggests that these kind of learners expect the programme to provide them with a set of competences that enhance their employability and provide them with expertise that is transferable and is relevant to the workplace. In contrast, those studying a DBA or EdD are likely to already have significant professional experience and are not therefore expecting the doctorate to add to this. They do, however, want a doctorate that relates to and draws upon this. Likewise, learners on these types of doctorates are more likely to begin the doctorate with existing expertise and the role of the programme in this case may be to consolidate and extend existing knowledge and skills and for some, validate professional experience.

The role that the doctorate occupies within a learner's career is explored further in the next chapter, which examines learners' trajectories and the effects of the doctoral learning process on them.

9
Identity

Introduction

Learning on professional doctorates takes different forms with programmes representing different ideas for different individuals. We have seen in the previous chapter that what the doctorate constitutes for students depends significantly on where the individual is in their particular career trajectory when they undertake the programme. In addition, we have seen that for some individuals the learning process represents a period of interaction and negotiation principally between themselves and the university (particularly in the case of the EdD); whereas for others, the research process is still governed by the university but industrial interests are also strongly represented.

In the previous chapter we focussed on learners' motivation for undertaking professional doctorates and different factors that influenced their decisions to undertake study at this highest level. This chapter examines how this learning impacts on the individual. Three areas are identified that reflect the way in which learning of this type influences the learner within their life-course and career trajectory, and these areas are: identity, experience and professional performance.

Identity

Learners regard the relationship between their self-identity and the professional doctorate in different ways, and each has particular consequences for the ways in which their identity is constructed. These relationships may take two forms: self-actualization, and social construction.

Self-actualization

The realization of personal potential and the ultimate goal of the individual as being self-actualization is a central component of the humanistic tradition; and Maslow (1954) identifies notions of self and personal growth as integral to his hierarchy of needs. In this relationship the learner's personal and professional selves are complexly intertwined; and in the case of the doctorate there is frequently a strong sense of personal investment. This is apparent in the extract below from an EdD graduate:

> Now at this point, that makes me middle fifties, and I couldn't move up the career ladder. I could have been a deputy head. I could have been a head teacher. Inside me, I know, I could have, but I missed out that big chunk and this is instead of that. This [the EdD] didn't enhance my career prospects. In fact, it produced a certain amount of resentment amongst senior managers that I was doing this. It came to light when we were *Ofsteded* in the school where I was and you had to put down what you were doing. You had to fill this big form in, and you had to put down what you were doing. And senior people who looked at it said 'well, we know you're doing a doctorate but you don't have to write it down'. In other words, I was rather threatening. I was threatening anyway because I was the former headteacher's wife. I'd never taught at the same school as him but they knew I was married to a headteacher. Now I was threatening because academically I was going to do something that nobody on that particular staff had, so I know I was threatening. I got no support in the sense, no time off, except I was allowed to have Fridays off to come to these conferences to get from the Isle of Man ('but don't dare be off on Monday!'). So I used to travel back overnight on Sunday night by boat and be at my desk by 9 o'clock in the morning. But the course was so satisfactory, so suitable for me, so riveting and it was making me *me*. I was doing something for me after years of doing things for other people, which I didn't mind because the things I was doing with the family and school were always good things but it wasn't me, and since I've finished the programme, I mean this is all personal, this isn't the programme itself, I feel as though I've won the lottery. No I don't, it's better than winning, its not winning the lottery because you couldn't win it on the lottery. I've done this for me. I didn't need anybody else's help for a leg up. I needed help from the staff here. I needed help, very profound support from family and friends who understood what I was doing, but I did it, I got it, I won it, its mine. I don't care whether it brings extra money in or any extra jobs, in fact it doesn't. I retired. I did it while I was full-time teaching, no time off, and only when the thesis went in, did I then hand my resignation in. And I handed it in because when I went to the deputy head and said 'I need three days off for the viva, I want to travel; one for the viva and one for the corrections'. I was told 'oh, can't you arrange it for half-term?' So I then handed my resignation in and the viva happened in the first term after I retired at the university's choice, because that's the way vivas have to be.

This learner conveys a sense of having 'missed out' professionally and the doctorate partly provides a way of compensating for her lack of professional recognition (see also Type 3 motivation discussed above). While she claims to be focusing on herself, she is also expressing a need to prove herself to her professional community and publicly demonstrate her achievement.

This desire for public and professional affirmation is also apparent in the extract below where an EdD graduate looks to the doctorate to validate his professional identity and experience. Here, he reflects on how he felt when this affirmation was not forthcoming:

> But the reaction at school wasn't particularly overwhelming, you know. I thought, 'Oh, God! This is an achievement.' I felt quite satisfied. I met some of the tutors there and we talked it all through. It was like a mark, the end of a stage, and I felt satisfied that I'd reached this level, not saying that it would help me in any way, particularly. I mentioned it at school and so on. But, there was no real kind of, 'Oh, well done!' or anything like that. The Head teacher was going through [a list of achievements], this was Christmas time, at the end of school do. She was mentioning a whole load of things that various teachers had done for the school, and achieved – sort of sporting activities. I thought, 'is she going to say anything about this?' And, it was getting toward the end of this list, and I thought, 'No, there's going to be nothing mentioned.' And, in fact, she didn't mention anything. And I thought, 'well, where does that fit then in her view of things?' And I went home feeling quite sort of down really.

This lack of external peer recognition was clearly an influential factor in the learner's sense of achievement. Whilst he did indeed feel some sense of personal accomplishment, this was tarnished and incomplete without public affirmation from his professional colleagues. The relationship between public and private aspects of a learner's identity is complex, and complementary, in that without any form of public affirmation, the private feeling of satisfaction experienced by the successful student is incomplete and as a consequence transitory. What can be considered privately satisfactory has to be understood in terms of what a society considers to be a worthwhile achievement; and public acknowledgement of this gives the individual some indication that their private good is publicly acceptable.

Peer reward is a continuing theme in the extract below from a DBA graduate who describes the value that he felt in having an opportunity to publicly share his work amongst his doctoral peers. This learning community and the peer support that it provides offers a safe environment in which to 'expose' the experience of learning, and in turn receive reassurance and encouragement:

> I'm the sort of person who could never do distance-learning because I'm an extrovert and I like interaction, and in a sense, what the course

gave me was a structure and a routine; and it meant I had to go there regularly. So, I scheduled it in. And what it did, it got me there talking to other people, thinking about the issues, going to theme groups, understanding what other people were doing. And it created a structure for doing that; that was very important to me, because, you know, I think that when you're doing something like a doctoral thesis, it's very lonely. And you go off and do it yourself. And I needed the regular pressure of going back to the university and showing what I was doing, and listening to other people, because it just kept me going. It was important being with a peer group. And with a peer group that was the same as me, I got, what did I get? Being part of a group. I didn't like it sometimes when other people seemed to be making more progress than me. It would spur me on.

Seeing himself in relation to and reflected in others provides a sense of security and of belonging. The following extract from an EdD graduate shows the importance of the learning community and highlights how isolating the learning experience can feel when this is not actively encouraged by the programme structure:

> And the funny thing was that the first part I was going on the modules, I felt really comfortable with everything, because I knew I was going to the next thing. There were people there, and then I felt shut-off where I was just doing it on my own, and that part I didn't really enjoy so much, I have to say, of the dissertation. I missed going up to the college and seeing everybody. So I felt that was quite a lonely stretch. And that's why I think I took so long on it, but, then in the end, it was going on so long, I was getting sick of it, and I wanted it to finish; and now I'm going through the stage of, 'well, what shall I do with my life?'

Learners in this self-actualization category are frequently experienced practitioners when they embark on their programme of study. This experience may in some cases consist of negative incidents that are directly linked to the individual's sense of self and how they relate to the doctorate. An example of this is presented below by an EdD graduate whose previous educational experiences played an important part in her undertaking the doctorate and subsequently affected her experiences on it:

> There were other reasons for doing it and one of them really goes way back. It will be interesting to see whether there are any other people who feel like as I do about having been children of the late fifties, who were subject to the 11+ and who didn't pass, and how that's left them feeling about their own capability, and how they need to prove themselves, and how they have to have recognisable markers that tell them that they're ok academically. And that certainly was an issue for me. I have a number of conversations from time to time with people here about the rule of the 11+ and grammar schools and all that sort of stuff.

And we tend to have quite different perspectives, because by and large they're all folks who passed and went through the system.

This graduate paints a negative picture of her own identity and strongly associates the doctorate with an opportunity for self-enhancement. Completion of the doctorate has been a way of demonstrating primarily to herself, that she is competent enough to achieve the highest of academic accolades. Confidence or rather a lack of it, is also implied and the experience of learning at this level and completing a programme of study is linked to the learner's own perception of their self-worth.

The examples in this section that show lack of confidence and a need for public affirmation have come from learners on EdD and DBA programmes, rather than EngD students who are less associated with this category of self-actualization. As we have seen from the previous chapter, those studying for the EngD are in most cases younger with less professional experience, and this perhaps implies that they have a stronger sense of self-worth and need a different level of external endorsement. These kinds of learners feature more prominently in the following category on social construction.

Social construction

The role that social experience occupies in constructing the self is associated with Mead (1964) who emphasizes the importance of the person seeing themselves reflected by others. The idea of the self being a social construction has a number of distinguishing characteristics in the context of a professional doctorate, the first of which is professional socialization. In this relationship the doctorate constitutes an important vehicle for shaping the learner's professional identity and for learners (many of whom are at an early stage in their career) to acquire workplace experience. The doctorate provides an environment in which an individual can develop and adopt a professional identity and become socialized into ways of operating that feature within their particular professional domain. This relationship is best exemplified by examining the experiences of EngD students, who, as we have already noted, are inducted into a training or apprenticeship model, which has the aim of preparing future engineering professionals. Here, an EngD student in the latter stages of their programme highlights the value gained from the cohort structure of the programme and the sense of community that he felt had been fostered. In this extract, the doctorate appears to enable learners to pool their varied experiences and collectively learn from these across the different project contexts:

At any stage of your project, you'll come up against certain issues, industrial, academic, project related, non-project related, whatever, but having a group of 10 or 15 people going through exactly the same experiences with you helps you consolidate your ideas about those kind of things as well as technical things as well. And I think that's very important for your professional side, learning how to deal with things professionally.

In addition to the value obtained from the student community experience, supervision was also considered to offer important opportunities for acquiring understanding in different professional domains.

In the next example, another EngD student discusses how joint supervision has effectively inducted her into both academic and professional worlds, or at least has enabled her to gain credibility in both settings. The implication of this is that without having a supervisor from both an academic and an industrial context, credibility in each site is compromised:

> That's what my supervisor is doing, he's very focused on making sure that I come out as a good PhD student, but the fact that I have an industrial supervisor that's there, saying what needs doing as well, that is what gives me the EngD. But I need them both, I feel I need that, I need to be academic in a way, it's not just for me, but for the company itself, because I'm going to carry this product into a volatile environment where it's going to be attacked by competitors. And the more rigorous the work that I've done, then the better the product will stand in the market. But the fact that I've done the quality, a qualitative academic study as part of this work, it's unlikely that anyone in industry is going to be able to question that, which gives the product a much better standard. My company has no female engineers, has never had a female engineer, and I've had a lot of resentment because of that. A lot of people have automatically assumed that I haven't got a clue what I'm talking about, then I open my mouth . . . and then they've sit there stunned, and I've had several comments: 'My God you can talk technical.' But you get used to that, that's part of the deal. But I think had I taken a PhD I would have been in trouble. There's little knots of people that have been in the industry for thirty odd years, I mean I'm the first. The closest doctor in the industry to me is forty-one, and I'm twenty-six. So there's quite a big age gap between us, and there was a big age gap between him and the next oldest one. Most of the work was done between 1960 and 1970, and that is the same today. Most people are retired, and there are a lot of barriers that you have to break down.

The lack of professional experience that this student has and the fact that this is in contrast to her professional colleagues, makes her more dependent on having the doctoral qualification as evidence that she is of a suitable calibre to perform in the workplace. The doctorate in this case is being used as a vehicle to break down the barriers that she refers to and compensate for how her age and gender is received in the workplace. Enhanced professional status features prominently in what this student expects from the experience of doing the doctorate and it is anticipated that the experience will provide a means of achieving accelerated career development.

Whilst the examples from learners on EngD programmes illustrate the way in which the doctorate is used for professional socialization for those in the early stages of their careers, there is a different relationship where the doctorate features later in a learner's professional life. In this case, the learner does not have the same expectation that the doctorate will provide an induction into a particular profession and its associated ways of working. For these individuals that are already established professionals with significant work experience, the transition to being a student signals the onset of a new period of socialization. For many professional doctorate students on DBA and EdD programmes, considerable time has often elapsed since their last experience of formal education. The expectations and requirements placed upon the individual as they take on a new student identity differ from those that the individual may be most familiar with in their workplace. Many may be used to occupying senior positions within their respective workplaces where responsibility and authority resides with them. The experience presented by the professional doctorate requires this to shift with consequences for where power resides. In the following extract from an EdD student, she demonstrates these multiple identities of 'professional' and 'student' and reflects on the transition from one to the other:

> Funnily enough, that really rang a bell because when I was driving up here, I actually put on my University scarf. When I was leaving work, this is probably really naff, but when I was leaving work, I was saying, 'I'm going to be a student now', as if it was a different world. And of course it is part of my life, but it's kind of boxing it up and saying, 'this is how I now become a student'. But I think that's probably the most difficult thing. I'm now in a more onerous job and therefore that's tricky. I probably had more time in work time before, so having the doctorate helped me get this higher job; but, at the same time, of course, it gives you less time to spend than you perhaps did. But the other thing with most of us is juggling our home lives. I mean, I have no children but I'm carer for my husband who has epilepsy. He's in work, but then again, you're forcing your priority onto someone else and it is quite tricky.

Students compartmentalize their study and professional lives, so that they develop different narratives for each. In addition, many of them also have to balance these against the demands made on them by their personal lives. These multiple identities are not easy to reconcile, and compartmentalization provides a way out of this dilemma.

Experiential learning

Experience is frequently used as a distinguishing characteristic of professional doctorates (Maxwell 2003b) both in terms of the nature of the population who are typically experienced professionals and the role that this experience occupies within such programmes. Experiential learning has been considered to be a key to adult forms of education or andragogy. Experience is understood as both the most important resource for learning and the foundation for developing new ideas and a new sense of self. It is characteristic of adults rather than children, because the latter are considered to have had less meaningful experiences. For students on professional doctorate courses, reflecting on their experience, is, in part, designed to give credibility to, and validate, it.

Usher *et al.* (1997) suggest, however, that experiential validation is flawed as a pedagogical approach. First, experience may be reified so that the learner is not encouraged or at least is not able to move beyond the limitations and boundaries of their experience. Second, experience is frequently not understood as culturally constructed, pre-interpreted and situated. This would suggest that there is a need to avoid reification of the learner's experience, and implement critical pedagogies to counterbalance the pre-interpreted nature of experience.

For learners, there are several ways in which the notion of experience is affected by the doctorate, which impacts upon the way in which experience is consequently conceptualized by the individual. For some, the professional doctorate provides an opportunity to revisit and re-evaluate existing experience. In some cases this requires a 'coming to terms' with previous events that have to date been difficult to reconcile. One of the roles that the doctorate occupied for the EdD graduate below was as a displacement activity for her failure to reach the highest level of her profession:

> I don't regret now not reaching higher up the profession, although there was a time when I used to sort of moan and groan and say 'you know, I've raised the children. I've been a good headteacher's wife.' I never said it and complained but I felt as though I could have done this. And yet all the men in my life, my sons, my husband, my father, have always been encouraging. I've never been 'the woman'. To my father, I was a child. I was educated just as much as the son. To my husband, I was an equal who was the only one who could look after our children, really, in those days.

For this individual the doctorate represented a position of closure. Through the doctorate she has been able to privately and publicly demonstrate a particular level of ability that she felt had not previously been recognized. This has acted as confirmation that she could have occupied a more senior professional role if she had chosen to pursue it. This relates to the notion of experiential validation whereby the doctorate represents a means of affirming or formally recognizing experience, though, as we noted above, this in itself creates problems.

A further difficulty with this concept of experiential validation arises when differing kinds of experiences occupy different statuses. Learners find that some experience that is given credence within their workplace is not valued to the same degree within an academic context. Earlier, we saw that learners' own experience occupies different roles within programmes, with some designed to draw heavily on learners' existing knowledge, and others placing greater emphasis on the acquisition of new knowledge. In the latter case the learner is forced to begin the programme as a 'student' with a canvas that does not necessarily reflect previous professional experience. Here, the learner is presented with a situation, which alters not only the role that they are used to occupying but also the status that is associated with it. Power and authority lie with the academic tutor as they impart new knowledge and ensure that learners acquire and demonstrate appropriate ways of operating. Particularly for EdD and DBA learners, many of whom possess substantial experience, they are encouraged to extend their experience through the academic process.

Acquiring new and formalized knowledge may lead learners to critique their own experience and perhaps for the first time to find it problematic. Relating and equating one's own lived experience with formalized knowledge, particularly when the validity of that experience is being questioned, has implications for how professional identity is perceived. For younger and less experienced learners, the relationship is less likely to be as complex because the doctorate will present an opportunity for acquiring and developing experience and a similar sense of professional self is unlikely to be as well-developed.

Professional performance

A contribution to or relationship with professional practice is clearly one of the defining features of a professional doctorate, but the extent to which the doctorate affects the learners' professional performance varies. The following example from an EdD graduate emphasizes the value in gaining a broader, contextual understanding of their practice that the doctorate has provided them with:

> I think it's given me a knowledge base, the one that I wanted, really, to go with the practice that I'd had and I feel that I'm more authoritative in the things that I'm saying, and people seem to respect my opinion more, so I don't have any of this nonsense of 'you don't know anything about education any more', because I can give it to them now in their terms. It definitely, I think, has made me more authoritative. It's got me into doing areas of work such as devising e-learning strategies and that kind of thing which I probably wouldn't have been involved with at all before, even though I had an interest in that, and was known to be interested. I didn't have the knowledge and the research that gave me the sort of right to be on that project. But to me, it's just given me permission to take time out in my own life, in my home life as it were, to prioritise learning about education and about the foundation for my job and it's been vindicated because I feel I've learned a huge amount. I don't know whether people ever come on higher degrees thinking they're going to

learn anything or whether they're going to impart stuff; but, to me, I wanted to learn as well as to impart and I have succeeded in that. I've learned masses of stuff, particularly a new way of thinking and that's maybe because of my professional background as a lawyer. I don't know whether you've found this as well, but, with law, your mode of thinking and learning is all to do with the small picture, the detail, the analytical, and here I'm having to go against my natural inclination and see the big picture all the time. And that has been tremendously good for me, not just professionally, but I think also as a person. I think I'm less boring, perhaps. I've got more to say on more things.

This is reiterated by a student on a DBA course:

I don't think I could have maintained the motivation because, in a sense, I wanted to see that there was an output for the work I was doing on my doctorate. In my case, I wouldn't say I was fortunate, but I certainly made sure that there were some fairly significant company-wide outputs on the work I was doing. I think the question is probably, in my case, would that work that I was doing have been done any differently if I hadn't done the doctorate, and I think the answer would have been 'yes'. It would have been done differently. It would have still been implemented but I think the knowledge, the point you make about the knowledge, that what I was doing was addressing the right type of issues, and was taking very much an international perspective rather than [a local one]. I'm working in the West Midlands in the UK and I'm doing this piece of work, actually looking at American practices, Japanese practices as part of the research process, very much bolstered, added to what I was doing, but certainly added to my own personal credibility.

The following extract from a DBA graduate highlights the changes that occurred within her practice throughout the doctorate:

So, actually doing my doctorate made a huge, huge impact on my work, very positive. And it wasn't like at the end, writing it up and giving it to people. It was happening all the way through. And because I was reading the literature, because I was developing these models. It was being used, and fed back, and it meant that actually my changed practice was so much better than it would have been if I'd just been doing it without doing the doctorate as well. Because I think that right now, I can feel that I'm more critical. Whenever I read any business proposal, I don't just take things at its face value. I always question their assumptions and say, 'where do you get this fact from'.

The following EdD student also stresses his use of a critical approach and how it has been developed during his doctoral experience:

I have very different views about educational psychology practice than I had only two or three years ago as a result of what I've gone through. I'm far more questioning now, far more penetrating and analytical about all sorts of things. But in a sort of friendly way. But I'm actually more, and I know how to sort of think round things a lot more than I used to. I'm not so accepting of old morals and traditional modes of working, and I have very clear ideas about new ways of working in line with moral understandings of psychology and education. And they put me in touch with that. So, I'm very different. I'm, professionally, a very different person from what I was at the start. I've moved a long, long way as a professional, not just in terms of how effective I can be but how I think about the profession of educational psychology.

The above extracts demonstrate the university's emphasis on trying to develop a sense of critical appraisal amongst learners on different types of doctorate. Inevitably approaches to this will vary across institutions and amongst the three types of doctorate, but it is clear that professional practice has been brought into question by this aspect of the doctorate. The extent to which learners can and are expected to critique their own practice or problematize their own experience varies according to the profile of the learner. Those studying EngDs for example will not have the same amount of experience on which to reflect as those registered on EdDs and DBAs.

Whilst the learners featured above emphasize the positive gains that critique can have, the following student highlights the more difficult workplace relationships that may result from adopting a more critical approach:

No longer do I sit and think, 'Oer', I actually say, 'there's another way of looking at this or have you thought of this?' and everyone goes quiet and gives me that look: 'You're not supposed to say that!' You know, all those sorts of things. So, actually on one level it's very liberating for me, but in a sense it also creates enormous tensions and difficulties with my colleagues because I'm no longer the easy-going, 'Yeah, all right' type but actually challenge things now. I challenge people. And they don't always like it. Some people do. The older members of the service don't like it so much as the younger ones. The ones that have been in it quite a long time. I can see that it does challenge them. I mean, it's not always easy for them. It's actually set me apart from my colleagues in one sense.

This sense of professional sidelining was not apparent in those learners who felt that they had achieved some form of promotion. In the case of the EdD learner below, promotion is real, although he is not certain that it was a direct consequence of pursuing the doctorate:

But I think a lot of the people that we met on the course and all these experts that came to give addresses and so on, and the presentations that we had to do, I think, did give me a bit more confidence when it came to some interviews. And if you're trying to relate career progression to the course, I did get a promotion onto the senior management team. But that was a couple of years into the course. And, of course, the head teacher knew I was doing this, but whether that helped or not, but it may have given me a bit more confidence to push myself forward.

In this case, the promotion is symbolic rather than actual as the DBA graduate below considers the title to have made a difference to his professional standing:

> The DBA gives me a better standing in the business world. I mean, with a doctor in front of your name, people give you the respect in your own field. I mean, that helps. Directly I don't think this is of any real benefit in terms of scope, expansion, or title, or promotion, and so forth.

These brief extracts reflect the concerns of students undertaking professional doctorate courses. Instrumentality comes in many guises, and here this student is suggesting that a doctorate may be valued for its status rather than as a means to improve practice or even to achieve promotion.

Conclusion

Learners' relationships with their doctorates occur at differing stages in their trajectories and we suggest that concepts of identity, experience and professional performance vary according to when this interaction occurs. A closer relationship was apparent between EdD/DBA learners and self-actualization, where we identified that concepts of personal investment, peer recognition and professional affirmation are strong features of the way in which these learners construct their identity in relation to the doctorate. As we have suggested previously, students on EdD and DBA programmes frequently possess substantial professional experience whereas those on EngDs are far more likely to be in the early stages of their careers. Concepts of self-identity for these EngD learners reflected this limited experience and were more strongly characterized by social construction. Here we saw that the notion of being inducted into a professional domain or set of workplace practices formed an important part of how their self-identity was shaped throughout the doctorate programme.

We have seen during the course of this chapter that for some learners, the doctorate presents a point of closure particularly for experience that has been previously unacknowledged. We also noted that placing lived experience under scrutiny can be problematic and the consequences of this appraisal can be a re-evaluation of professional judgement and integrity. We now move from the individual learner to explore broader, contextual issues concerning the doctorate, status hierarchies and professionalism. Given the varied histories and origins of these different programmes, it is likely that views of knowledge and understandings of the relationships between academic and practitioner knowledge will differ accordingly.

10

The Professions: Status and Qualifications

Introduction

Lee *et al.* (2000), in an attempt to distinguish between first generation and second generation professional doctorates, provide a model of a hybrid curriculum that combines three interrelated elements: the university, the workplace and the profession. They describe this hybrid model as 'a three-way model, where the university, the candidate's profession and the particular work-site of the research meet in specific and local ways, in the context of a specific organisation' (127). The different elements of the hybrid curriculum therefore coalesce in different ways, resulting in the development by the student of forms of knowledge, where the hybridity resides in the sourcing of that knowledge. Previously, we discussed in some detail the relationship between the university and the workplace, and the various hybrid forms of knowledge developed as a consequence (see Chapter 4). The missing dimension is the profession, and in this chapter we consider the role of the professional doctorate in relation to participants' status, qualifications and their professional identity.

This depiction of the hybrid curriculum is not without its problems. The first of these is that it implies an equal role for each of the elements. This is problematic because the professional doctorates, that have been developed or are in the process of being developed, have incorporated the professional element, and reference to professional concerns, in different ways. The second problem, related to this, is that professionality is a contested concept. In other words, though an occupation may strive for professional status and designation, this may not be accepted or even endorsed by other groups, occupations or even internally, by members of the body itself.

Elliott and Hughes (1998) suggest that an occupation has to have acquired the following characteristics for it to call itself a profession: an ideal of service, the formation of a professional community, the development of an epistemology of practice, the designation of a degree of autonomy and independence, and a code of ethics. By ideal of service, they mean that a profession has a moral basis to it and a set of ideals, which are then applied in the practice setting. The type of knowledge produced in and for the practice focuses on both means and ends, and is different from a technicist view where practitioners are merely concerned with determining a measure of technical efficiency, that will necessarily lead to the achievement of pre-determined ends and these are separate from the determination of means *per se*. This implies a degree of autonomy, and the production of a type of good that is beneficent; that is, the good necessarily has to involve improvements to the lifestyle and opportunities of a distinct clientele group.

Their second characteristic is the development of a professional community engaged on similar activities. Associated with this is the formation of a discourse community, which in turns implies a common commitment to a specific epistemology of practice. This last then is Elliott and Hughes's third characteristic, and they mean by it that a profession shares a common view of what type of evidence is appropriate for the conduct of their business; how that evidential base is used; and the designation of boundaries to exclude forms of evidence and reasoning that are alien to the practice.

Elliott and Hughes's fourth characteristic of a profession is that it has a specified degree of autonomy and independence. It is self-regulating, in so far as it has developed a code of practice consisting of rules and the means and infrastructure to enforce those rules. Furthermore, it has a degree of autonomy from the state, including what Whitty (2001) describes as a 'professional mandate', which, though in a state of continuous negotiation and renegotiation, is a bargain with the state that determines the degree of independence and autonomy it can claim.

The final characteristic that Elliott and Hughes identify for a profession is a code of ethics. This in turn is dependent on the particular epistemology of practice and type of discourse community that currently exists within the profession. However, it also suggests that members are required to abide both by the rules of the profession, enforced by the imposition of sanctions, and by a set of informal specifications for how a member of that profession should behave.

There are two problems with this definition of a profession. The first is that the degree of autonomy negotiated between the profession and the state is always subject to renegotiation at different times and in different ways, so that whether an occupation at any one time has the requisite amount of autonomy to qualify as a profession is a difficult matter to determine. The teaching profession for example, has been called a quasi-profession because it has failed to meet the strict definition of autonomy some people are prepared to apply. The second problem is the extent to which the professional designation embraces all the activities of members of that profession. So, for example, Whitty (2001) refers to the way different elements of a profession may be developing different forms of professionalism with consequently different relations to the state.

However, there is a more profound difficulty, and this refers to the changing ideological dimension of professionality. As Hanlon (1998) suggests, professions were characterized by an ideal of beneficence in which the professional expert was trusted to work in the best interests of the clientele body. This, he argues, has been partly replaced by a 'commercialized professionalism', where the search for profitability and international competitiveness has meant that some clients are privileged over others. The professional body is therefore fragmenting, and attempts to designate some occupations as professions and others as not becomes even more difficult. This, however, has not exhausted the currency of professionalism, or even of attempts by specific occupations to engage in processes of professionalization (Whitty 2001), as it is possible to understand it in an active sense, as the profession seeking status and influence and the rewards that accompany it. That is, we should understand the use of the term itself as a move by members of particular occupations to extend their power and influence, to bolster their particular epistemological position, and to cement in place the ideological apparatus for their continued existence. One part of this strategy is the development of a professional doctorate so that recognition of achievement by a university both accredits learning for the individual and bestows status on the profession to which the individual belongs.

The role of professional doctorates in the professions

Professional doctorates have emerged in the UK at a time when there is not only a mass expansion of higher education, but there are also substantial changes in the ways that professional occupations are educated and organized. These changes include the growing number of professions which now require graduate or even postgraduate status, the introduction of mandatory continuing professional development for a growing number of professions, and the requirements for the revalidation of a licence to practise; this last being contingent on continuing professional development, and the increased complexity of professional roles. Thus 'the complexities of employment in the modern world require a high level of intellectual sophistication, and this has generated pressure for higher qualifications' (UKCGE 2002: 17).

In addition to these factors there has been the growth of the 'competence' movement, related in the UK largely to the National Vocational Qualifications initiative, and now replaced by occupational standards. This has led to greater transparency and accountability for professional qualifications, and has resulted in a greater demand for higher-level qualifications. In the case of the professions, level 5 NVQs were introduced as a concept for postgraduate progression, leading to a demand for higher professional development. In this context, Bourner *et al.* suggest a number of reasons for the growth of professional doctorates, principal amongst which is:

> the inevitable consequence of a drift towards vocationalism. From this perspective, the rise of professional doctorates is evidence that by the

1990s the competencies approach had at last reached the highest, doctoral, level in England.

(2001a: 78)

Professional bodies have tried over time to link their assessment to the actual demands of the occupation concerned, and develop sophisticated analyses of the knowledge, skill and competence requirements for professional activities. These have frequently been based on detailed functional analysis of what individual professionals actually do in the workplace, and have now been linked to the work carried out by National Training Organisations. While there has been considerable opposition from both universities and the professions to the competency movement and the concept of NVQs, largely on the grounds that they appear to underplay the importance of high level understanding and professional judgement, this has been largely overtaken in universities by the concept of learning outcomes.

Barnett criticises the move to define professional education in terms of competences and learning outcomes, and suggests that:

a genuine higher education for the professions will not be content with reflecting the professionally defined competences but will insert modes of reasoning, action and reflection into the curriculum.

(1994: 11)

It is for this reason that professional doctorates have sought to provide forms of higher professional development and learning within a framework of rigorous reflection and intellectual demand. However, professional doctorates appeared at a time when external bodies such as the Quality Assurance Agency introduced the requirement that university programmes should be accompanied by clear learning outcomes; this occurred around the time that requirements began to be made that the PhD should also develop generic and transferable competencies and skills, and at a time when employers were also making demands for generic skills of their senior as well as other employees. This therefore mandated professional doctorates to develop higher-order competences or 'meta-competences' to assist the professional in moving beyond the immediate, time- and context-bound work setting, standing back and taking an enhanced professional perspective on the work.

However, perhaps one of the greatest changes in Higher Education in this area has been the trend, principally but not only, within the health area for professional qualifications, to move from the field to the university, that is to move from an apprenticeship model with accreditation and licensing by a professional body to a model where the university delivers education and training, and forms a partnership with a professional body in relation to professional accreditation and licensing. This has occurred in medical fields such as physiotherapy, podiatry, occupational therapy and other professions, within what were the *Professions Allied to Medicine* (now *Professions Supplementary to Medicine*), which were, until recently, regulated within the CPSM (Council for Professions Supplementary to Medicine) and are now regulated within the Health Professions Council. These changes have led to under-graduate degree level qualifications for the professions supplementary to medicine, and to professional doctorate level qualifications for their teachers, now based within the academy. Thus before 1976 all physiotherapy pre-registration coures were based in NHS schools, and the final qualifcation was a diploma awarded by the Chartered Society of Physiotherapy (CSP). During the 1970s, these schools began to move into higher education institutions with a Bachelor degree (BSc) as the final qualification. The BSc was introduced in 1976, though it was not until 1992 that physiotherapy became an all-graduate profession, with BSc (Hons) the final qualification, and also conferring the licence to practise through recognition by the Chartered body.

The shift of professional education and training to Higher Education has led to a new professional group, university educators of professions allied to medicine, of whom a significant number have acquired their qualification through the professional doctorate, in particular the EdD. Thus, there has been both an expansion within higher education of degree level qualifications which simultaneously entitle graduates to the licence to practise, hitherto the exclusive preserve of a professional body, and also a substantial increase in academic staff required to teach these entrants to the profession, who themselves were in need of professional qualifications:

> Professional higher education builds partnerships and alliances inside and outside of the academy . . . The decision by the National Health Service (NHS) to shift the majority of its training for professionals other than doctors into the higher education sector is an excellent test case of . . . tensions and potential rewards in action. In this context, the 'service' (represented by health authorities, trusts and purchasing consortia) will want . . . an enhanced reputation for the various careers involved (leading ideally to high recruitment and retention).
>
> (Watson 2000: 7)

Universities have worked in collaboration with professional and statutory bodies 'with a resulting upgrade of both entry-level and continuing professional development (CPD) courses in terms of their attractiveness and the standards achieved' (Watson 2000: 10). In addition, with degree inflation over the past decade, a number of professions have enhanced their own qualifications and used these to raise their status.

The clearest example of the evolution and enhancement of qualifications in relation to status is that provided by clinical psychology in the UK. The first formally recognized course in clinical psychology was a one-year diploma course that started in 1947. This Diploma course was extended and designated a Masters course during the 1960s, further extended to a duration of three years, and finally in the late 1980s changed to a doctoral level course, the DClinPsy. These developments have been led in large measure by the profession itself and its professional body, the British Psychological Society (BPS), which has responsibility for the accreditation of professional qualifications and for setting the standards and requirements for the licence to practise. At the time of the change to doctoral status, there was a view within the profession and its professional division within the British Psychological Society that the profession of clinical psychology was undervalued and under-remunerated, particularly in comparison with medical colleagues working alongside them within the National Health Service, whose duration of initial qualification was the same (Donn *et al.* 2000). Enhancement of the nature and level of qualification was one way to address this perceived status issue. Following the move to universal doctoral level entry to the profession of clinical psychology across the UK, and a perceived greater parity with medical doctors, already qualified clinical psychologists expressed the need to have doctoral level qualifications, with the result that 'top-up' doctorates (professional doctorates also named DClinPsy) were developed for mid-career professionals to enhance their qualifications and status.

In addition to an enhanced initial qualification, a number of professions have introduced mandatory continuing professional development, often as part of the revalidation of the licence to practise (cf. Becher 1999a). For example the Council for Professions Supplementary to Medicine (CPSM) transformed by legislation to become the Health Professions Council (HPC) in 2002, now requires the 12 professions (clinicians such as occupational therapists) which are registered with the Council to engage in CPD as part of the requirements for the licence to practise.

Most traditional professions define competence through the possession of a certain level of qualification, adherence to a professional code of ethics (which includes a commitment to maintain competence and not to practise beyond one's competence), and agreement to abide by disciplinary procedures.

According to traditional accounts of professionalism, 'the validation of professional practice and public trust is implicit in the notion of professional status, or through the "licence to practise" awarded by the professional body at the time of professional qualification or recognition' (Lunt 2002: 7). Recent well-publicized cases of professional negligence and incompetence in the medical and other professional fields have served to undermine public trust and have led the government to call for tighter curbs on professional autonomy, in particular in relation to self-regulation. Thus, for the General Medical Council (GMC), revalidation or re-accreditation is a major issue:

> In 1999 we decided that registration should become an up-to-date statement of each doctor's fitness to practise . . . Revalidation is part of a wider form of medical regulation. There is a generally recognised need for a new approach to professionalism in medicine and health care, a culture which promotes quality improvement, recognised the inevitability of error in a judgement-based discipline like medicine, and encourages – in the interests of patients – openness and honesty about the performance of clinical teams and individual health professionals.
>
> (GMC 2000: 5)

With governments interested in the effectiveness of self-regulation, a number of other professions have taken seriously the concept of current 'fitness to practise' and have made revalidation of the practising certificate or licence to practise contingent on mandatory continuing professional development. This has led to a number of professions (for example pharmacy) developing professional doctorates which both enhance the current competence of practitioners and which also encourage self-reflection and self-awareness within a critical framework of doctoral study (cf. Boud and Walker 1998). Each of the three professional doctorates examined in this book (the DBA, the EdD and the EngD) have different professional histories, and students undertaking them understand the professional element and the place and role of their profession differently.

The business doctorate

The MBA served for many years as the professional qualification in the field of business or management, and numbers of graduates exceeded those on other Masters courses. There has been a range of efforts to professionalize the field of management, including seeking membership of the body of managers in the United Kingdom Inter-Professional Group, the federal body that brings together the professional bodies of the major professions within the UK. Although the DBA is frequently a progression from the MBA, and the majority of entrants to the DBA have already obtained an MBA, the motivation for registration most frequently expressed by DBA participants and graduates was 'intrinsic personal/professional affirmation' (see Chapter 7), and the DBA does not appear to be subject to degree or credential inflation, perhaps because of the diffuse and indeterminate nature of business and related fields in terms of professional identity.

One programme leader described the views of the Principal of the College in the following way:

> He commented on how impressed he was with the quality of the people. He said that they were all committed to finding things out, improving themselves and sorting something out in their mind. Many had been holding down major development jobs and wanted the opportunity to step back from this and have a framework in which they could study. He thought that the students' motivation was not about getting a qualification to improve their career, because the career by and large has been established, but much more to do with an interest in a particular subject and the support of an institution in helping them achieve the things they want to achieve. Another supervisor made the point that whereas the aim of many MBA students is connected to the development of their career path, the DBA students are more concerned with the programme as intellectual stimulus. Some are in their fifties and sixties and are not seeking any direct career enhancement out of their doctorate but want personal development.

However, one university which offers a DBA programme claims that it is designed to both give maximum credibility, and open doors into academic life, consultancy or senior executive positions. A DBA student clearly saw the opportunity for upgrading:

> I guess it's a follow-on to my pursuit in trying to upgrade myself. I've been constantly upgrading myself through external courses, and after completing (my Masters) I was thinking that now, since I've been interested in pursuing management studies and so forth, it's probably worth while for me to take on another goal, to achieve something. It's not a means to an end, but, more. Since I'm upgrading myself, I might as well pursue a qualification.

Another graduate saw the DBA as a 'kind of business credential':

> I'm a chartered engineer, all that wonderful stuff, and yet really since 1974 I've been a technocrat operating in a business environment, and as I've moved on in years and at least in X Company terms reaching the mandatory retirement age of 60 (I'm actually 56 just for the record); now my view was that, on the basis that I'm not a retiring sort of person, that I'd like to get some kind of business credential. That reinforces what I've done over so many years.

It was clear from a number of the interviews with DBA graduates that the DBA degree had given them additional status, credibility, and an enhanced sense of competence. The benefits to their profession are indeterminate, and difficult to quantify. Yet it is being suggested here that credentialing is not just about acquiring specific skills and competences in order to make the acquirer a better practitioner in the workplace, it is also about gaining status, having greater credibility, and ultimately, changing the public perception of the core business. The business profession, even though diffuse and indeterminate, benefits from its members being seen as professional and indeed competent. Raising the level of academic award achieved by its members contributes to this changing perception.

The education doctorate

As we suggested above, the education profession is fragmented, and includes individuals who work in a number of very different settings and who are members of a number of different bodies, some of which are professional associations. The professionalization of teachers has been the subject of much recent debate, and the formation of the General Teaching Council (GTC) has been heralded by some as constituting a significant step in that direction.

The GTC Code of Professional values and practice for teachers states that:

> Teachers entering the teaching profession in England have been trained to a professional standard that has prepared them for the rigours and

realities of the classroom. They understand that maintaining and developing their skills, knowledge and expertise is vital to achieving success. They take responsibility for their own continuing professional development, through the opportunities available to them, to make sure that the pupils receive the best and most relevant education. Teachers continually reflect on their own practice, improve their skills and deepen their knowledge. They want to adapt their teaching appropriately, to take account of new findings, ideas and technologies.

(GTC 2002)

The EdD provides both the opportunity for teachers to reflect on their practice, to learn from and research their practice, and to gain advanced qualifications in an increasingly credential-based world of work. So, for one EdD student:

I decided to do a doctorate rather than a Master's because it seemed to me if I was going to spend 3 years studying I may as well spend four and get a doctorate. I wanted that extra bit of status, I think.

Another EdD graduate expressed her feelings after graduating from the EdD:

the EdD gives me a greater feeling of being a professional, you know, it's a bit about status, but more about quality, about being a doctoral level professional. The ability to reflect on my practice, to research my professional work, to stand back and develop a critical stance, it has made all the difference to the way that I feel about my work, and the way that I am viewed by other people. Now they kind of respect me, I feel. I wonder what difference it would make to teachers' feelings of being professional if they all had to do doctorates.

The teaching profession, in comparison with the business and engineering professions has a greater stake in enhancing its professional profile with the general public, because its core business cannot be carried out without the direct approbation of parents who send their children to schools to be educated. In the fields of business and engineering, it is the product and not the producer that is under immediate scrutiny by the public.

Dale (1989) suggests that some professions have a licensed form of autonomy, whilst others have a regulated form of autonomy. The teaching profession, though granted considerable licence in the past, has increasingly been subject to various forms of regulation. As Whitty (2001) suggests, this creates something of a paradox, as the introduction in the UK of a General Teaching Council would seem to suggest reversion back to a form of licensed autonomy. This seeming paradox only begins to make sense when one considers that regardless of the degree of autonomy practised by the professions in the past, the state has in recent times redefined its role in relation to the professions. Neave (1988: 11) has coined the term 'the evaluative state' and he means by this that there has been 'a rationalization and wholescale redistribution of functions between center and periphery such that the center maintains overall strategic control through fewer, but more precise, policy levers including the operationalisation of criteria relating to "output quality" '. In Chapter 2, we made reference to this notion of the evaluative state, and suggested that it was having a profound effect on the way universities were conducting their business; here, we are suggesting that the key determinant of professional status, indeed whether an occupation could be considered to be a profession, was its degree of autonomy from state institutions. The education profession in the UK is now regulated in a number of ways, not least through inspection. It is too early to determine whether the introduction of the General Teaching Council will lead back to a more meaningful form of licensed autonomy.

The engineering doctorate

The engineering profession illustrates successfully the effect of enhanced qualifications and the role of the professional doctorate in developing the status of the profession. During the 1970s there was increasing pressure on the three-year Bachelor degree courses that constituted engineering undergraduate education; this pressure resulted from a growing need for the inclusion of a component of business and management studies in order to equip the graduate for employment as engineers. The result of this pressure was the development of four-year BEng courses, in part, as a result of the Finniston Report *Engineering our Future* (1980). The BEng evolved into the MEng in 1986, and the four-year integrated course was endorsed by the Engineering Council (the professional body), in that it provided the academic prerequisites for Professional Engineer status. The EngD builds on this by including a high-level integrated engineering programme, with at least one university enabling participants to take the MBA as the first part of the EngD, in order to develop rounded, high flying engineers.

One of the university tutors describes its evolution in the following way:

> An extended or enhanced undergraduate programme, which became the four year MEng, Master of Engineering, an undergraduate degree, a four year undergraduate, the first of the four year programmes. Many programmes have now gone to four years, because of the increase of the body of knowledge that has to be taught, plus the fact that there's obviously concern from the profession. Now there was a need for an EngD as the next qualification.

We have already noted that the engineering profession played a larger role in the development of professional doctorates than was the case with the education and business doctorates, and that the engineering profession is less diffuse. In this context, the EPSRC statement of aims and objectives in Best Practice Notes, includes the following:

EngD ... should provide graduates with the ability to innovate and implement new ideas in practice, and enable them to reach senior positions in industry early in their careers.

This reinforces the idea of a unitary self-regulating body that has credibility amongst its members. This is reflected in the high status accorded to the doctorate by participants and other members alike. For example, one EngD research engineer claimed: 'It will definitely boost your career having a doctorate'; while another graduate stated that:

I realised I wasn't going to get much further without getting some more qualifications, and the EngD seemed the best way to improve myself and get the recognition I wanted. I had the opportunity to continue my professional development. I've now got my chartered engineer status and get a doctorate qualification at the same time. And that's basically why I did it.

And a current research engineer suggests an added international dimension to the status that the doctorate will give him:

I work in the Netherlands and Germany. What I would like to do is climb the corporate ladder as high as possible. And in countries like the Netherlands and in Germany, you need the doctorate.

The level of status gained by a profession is not a fixed commodity, but is subject to changes to the nature of the work undertaken by members of that profession, changes to the 'professional mandate' negotiated with governments, and the success or otherwise of the professional body to persuade the public of the professionality of their enterprise. One part of this strategy is the development of high-level qualifications for its members, taught and accredited by the universities.

Conclusion

We suggested at the beginning of this chapter that the process of professionalization requires five processes actively to be progressed: the development of an ideal of service, the active formation of a professional community, the development of an epistemology of practice, the negotiation with the state of an acceptable degree of autonomy, and the implementation of a code of ethics. We have also noted how the three different doctorates have been more or less successful in this. This is in part because they have different structural and institutional arrangements, in part because of the different arrangements they have made with the state, and in part because of the nature of the work (and its consequent epistemological orientation) that constitutes its core business.

In the concluding chapter, we draw together the themes and ideas that we have been developing throughout this book.

11

Conclusions: Hybrid Forms of Knowledge

Introduction

Professional doctorates have emerged out of and in competition with academic doctorates; in particular, the PhD. Comparisons between them are therefore inevitable, not least in that the PhD has been treated as the gold standard against which the professional doctorate has had to measure itself. If the professional doctorate is framed as an alternative set of teaching and learning practices but with similar outputs, then the products of each are comparable. However, if they embrace different types of knowledge-construction, then comparing the two becomes problematic. We have seen that the different professional doctorates are structured, taught and assessed in different ways, and that they vary between institutions, programmes, types, and even, given the developmental nature of the professional doctorate, between cohorts within the same institution and programme. We have also seen how the PhD, though in a state of constant evolution, comprises a different type of study, and indeed this is what one would expect, given that the one emerged from the other. Rationales for introducing professional doctorates range from developing a new relationship with the world of work, to attracting a new segment to the market for higher degree study, to repackaging the promotion of higher degree study so that a new type of person is attracted to what is still essentially a PhD, or to a genuine dissatisfaction with the narrow purpose and scope of the PhD. Possible models for distinguishing between PhDs and professional doctorates are inevitably post-hoc rationalizations for more pragmatic decisions made by universities. However, though these distinctions may appear trivial, the development of professional doctorates represents a trend away from a model of teaching and learning that is encapsulated in PhD study. Furthermore, the nature of PhD study has not remained static, as developments in its structure, delivery and target audience means that it is beginning to embrace some of the dimensions of first generation professional doctorates.

In Australia where the professional doctorate has been long established, a distinction is now drawn between first generation and second generation professional doctorates (Maxwell 2003a). Though this distinction is in part historical, in that second generation professional doctorates have been developed at a later point in time to first generation professional doctorates, it is more than this and reflects a radical break between the two. In other words, the latter both come after the former and are conceptually and procedurally different. In the UK, which started developing professional doctorates at a later point in time, some of these conceptual distinctions have been incorporated into single generation professional doctorates, and the distinction between first and second generation professional doctorates has less credibility. However, within the single generation model in the UK distinctions are drawn between high status and low status professional doctorates, usually for the same reasons as distinctions are drawn between first and second generation doctorates in Australia. The difference is that in the former case the older and better established model of writing and study has greater credibility, whereas in Australia this model is now genuinely being problematized.

It is therefore important for us to discuss what these distinctions might be, with the understanding that they represent actual and possible models for professional doctorate study. They relate to the use of portfolios as an alternative to the submission of a thesis or dissertation; the use of a variety of inscriptive practices as an alternative to writing for a single audience, such as the academic community; criteria for determining the quality of the product that are workplace-based rather than academically-orientated; a focus on a multiplicity of discourse communities rather than a single discourse community such as the academy; accreditation of professional knowledge rather than accreditation of academic knowledge; and pedagogies that embrace multiple sites of learning rather than single sites of learning, as in a traditional university-based course.

Portfolios

The portfolio, as the product for assessment and accreditation, has been enthusiastically endorsed for a number of reasons (Usher 2002). The first reason is that it provides a means by which a number of different pieces of work with different styles and intended for different audiences can be collected together for assessment purposes. One of the tacit criteria for assessment of a thesis is consistency of purpose, which in effect means that the piece is either written for a single audience; or that it conforms to the tenets for written work within a single discourse community; or that a single argument is sustained throughout; or that it maintains an integral form. The portfolio has a degree of flexibility so that different types of writing can be included, produced for different audiences, embracing different discourse communities, and because they are separate pieces, there is no need for any integrating device to draw them together. A compromise on some professional doctorate programmes exists whereby a number of disparate pieces of work are included but they are loosely integrated into a whole by the insertion of a commentary. This commentary of whatever length may be chronological, autobiographical, conceptual or developmental. The structure of a portfolio therefore allows a greater possibility of work being submitted for assessment which embraces both academic and workplace concerns, and therefore has the potential to weaken the boundaries between academic and professional discourse communities, a matter that has been of much concern within this book.

The second area of advantage that a portfolio has over a dissertation or thesis relates to the contentious area of progression within the professional doctorate. The taught courses may be assessed to a single standard or in terms of a progressive sequence of standards. With the former, students are expected to meet the standards of doctoral work at the beginning of the course; with the latter they are expected to reach doctoral standard at a later point in the course and some allowance is made during the earlier stages to accommodate the differential development of students' conceptual and writing skills. If a progressive element is built into the assessment design, this may be achieved by early taught units being marked to a lower standard than later ones (restricted progression), by the setting of different standards for different parts of the course (hierarchical progression), or by the completion by students of a portfolio of work at the end of the taught part of the course which meets the requirements for doctoral study (portfolio progression). Restricted progression requires the assignation of two different standards (logically related to each other); hierarchical progression requires a number of different standards (still logically related to each other, but at different levels of difficulty and numerous or restricted depending on the scale of the hierarchy); and portfolio progression requires one standard to be met by students at the end of the course.

These different types of progression indicate weak or strong (Bernstein 1990) boundaries between academic and practitioner knowledge. If students are expected to operate at doctoral level from the beginning of the course, then the boundaries between academic and practitioner knowledge are being constructed as strongly delineated, sacrosanct, not open to negotiation and impermeable. Indeed, we can go further than this, and suggest that practice knowledge is here being understood as inferior to academic knowledge and that the practitioner should therefore divest themselves of that knowledge and replace it with academic knowledge. On the other hand, if various forms of progression are built in, then weaker boundaries between academic and practitioner knowledge are being proposed. Progression comprises the ability of the student to access particular recognition and realization rules (cf. Bernstein 1990) to meet the requirements of the course; that is, students need to access these rules as they are defined by the university (though different universities will define them in different ways) and cross the divide between practitioner and academic communities of knowledge. Those rules comprise in part recognition by the student of the standards they are expected to meet at each stage of the course and the way assessment procedures structure their learning experiences. A portfolio structure allows a measure of progression to be built into the course. It also allows the submission of work that reflects the needs of different audiences. It is therefore polysemic in orientation.

Knowledge criteria

We have referred here to the relation between academic and workplace knowledge; and the way portfolio assessment has the potential to solve the problem of progression and therefore one of the problematic aspects of learning on professional doctorate courses. However, though portfolios in their purest form have this advantage, they do not in themselves resolve the issue of different criteria being applied by different assessors as to the quality of the work being produced. There are a number of possibilities here.

Various sets of criteria have been developed to allow researchers and readers of research to determine what is good research. Classical sets of criteria referred to the representativeness of the account. Thus an account was judged in terms of: its internal validity (whether experimentally the effects observed as a result of the intervention were actually caused by it and not by something else); external validity (whether findings from the case being investigated could be generalized to other cases in time and place); and objectivity (whether the preconceptions and biases of the researcher had been accounted for in the construction of the account and eliminated as influencing variables).

Guba and Lincoln (1985) suggested alternative criteria, though these were criticized for not being alternative or radical enough. They were: credibility (whether respondents agreed that the researcher had adequately represented their constructions of reality); transferability (whether the readers of the research agreed that the conclusions reached related usefully to settings which they themselves were immersed in); dependability (whether the researcher had been able to identify his/her effects during fieldwork and discount them); and confirmability ('the key question here is whether the data are qualitatively confirmable; in other words, whether the analysis is grounded in the data and whether inferences based on the data are logical and of high utility' (Guba and Lincoln 1985: 323)).

Guba and Lincoln were criticized for suggesting that there was a correct method, which, if properly applied, would lead to a correct account of reality. In an attempt to distance themselves from this perspective, Guba and Lincoln (1989) developed a further set of criteria: fairness (equal consideration should be given to all the various perspectives of participants in the research); educative authenticity (good research involves participants in the process of educating themselves); catalytic authenticity (this is where the research process has stimulated activity and decision-making); and empowerment (participants are now in a better position to make real choices about their professional activity).

Hammersley (1992) has suggested another framework: plausability/ credibility (whether the evidential claims are plausible or credible to the reader of the research); coherence (whether evidence and argument logically cohere); intentionality (whether a study is credible in terms of its stated intentions); and relevance (whether the research findings are relevant to issues of legitimate public concern). Evers and Lakomski (1991), arguing from a position of coherentist realism, suggest that research should be judged by whether it observes the virtues of simplicity, consistency, coherence, comprehensiveness, conservativeness and fecundity.

These sets of criteria overlap with each other and each in turn prioritizes one of the core principles (representativeness, coherence, change) over the others. Proponents of each seek to construct an argument based round whether the research text: is representative; corresponds with some external reality; is validated by respondents from the research setting; is grounded in the data; successfully changes what is; is consistent and coherent; is relevant in some specified way; or surfaces underlying power relations in the research setting and as a consequence repositions players in the game. Readers and assessors of research texts are therefore likely to bring different criteria to bear on how they read it and on how they make a judgement about its validity. Practitioners, for example, are likely to focus on its usefulness to their own practice; other researchers, depending on the frameworks they adopt for their own research, may focus on its representativeness and so on. Indeed, what is crucial in terms of the judgement that is made are those frameworks. Though much disputed, these constitute academic criteria.

Workplace criteria have been construed differently. Taylor (2003) suggests a number of criteria (adapted from Winter *et al.* 2000) that take us some way beyond the academic criteria listed above. The first of these is intelligibility – this relates to the audience for which it is intended and is a determinant of whether that audience can understand what is being proposed. The second is credibility, and this is defined by reference to its audience, so that this audience believes that the knowledge being produced is viable, that audience may of course be a practitioner one. The third criterion is immediacy, and this refers to the relevance of that knowledge in relation to present challenges and concerns in the workplace. The fourth criterion is originality, and by this is meant that the knowledge provides a new way of thinking about a specific problem or a new approach to practice. The fifth criterion is viability. Here, the work is judged by whether it has practical application in the workplace, and can progress the purposes and functions of the workplace. Finally, there is ethicality, where consistency is sought with the ethical practices of the community to which this knowledge is related. These six criteria take the framing of practitioner knowledge some way beyond those of academic knowledge. However, many of them are redolent of academic criteria, and they do not constitute a radical break with them.

Taylor (2003: 34) offers a further set of criteria that are more radical. The first of these is cost-effectiveness, and a product is judged by whether it meets this criterion. The second, scalability, refers to the ease with which the solution can be scaled up or down in its application. The third, integratability, refers to whether the knowledge/solution can be readily integrated into current operations. If it cannot and as a result requires significant retooling, it is not considered to have fulfilled this criterion. The fourth, exclusivability, refers to whether the knowledge/solution can be exploited as an exclusive resource for the organization. The fifth is timeliness, and refers to whether the knowledge/solution is developed on time. If the candidate has the capacity for meeting deadlines, then they are deemed to have fulfilled this criterion. Finally, Taylor suggests two forms of marketability. The first of these is internal to the organization, and refers to whether the knowledge/solution is politically and/or organizationally acceptable. The second of these is external, and this refers to whether the knowledge/solution, or its use, is acceptable to external stakeholders; in other words, 'does it offer potential "collateral benefits" in terms of market share, market position, market image (for the organisation and/or industry), etc.?' (Taylor 2003).

Earlier we suggested in relation to our discussion of different forms of hybrid knowledge that colonization can occur when a mode of knowledge becomes so powerful that it effectively subsumes another mode of knowledge. Here, we have an example with workplace criteria assuming such a dominant role that academic criteria become subservient. Indeed, this points to the difficulty of bridging academic and workplace settings, as the forms of colonization, whichever direction they take, imply either a weakening of the infrastructure of the academy or the ascription of workplace practices as inefficient, unproductive and regressive. The middle ground would suggest dissolution of the boundaries between the two sites of knowledge construction, and the creation of new forms of knowledge that satisfy both. The tensions between the two, certainly with regards to the development of professional doctorates in the UK, are as yet unresolved.

Inscription

The third distinction that has been made is in terms of different genres for writing. Traditional doctorates have conformed to a particular style of writing that may loosely be called academic. This has a number of characteristics that distinguish it from report writing to governing bodies for example, or poetic forms of writing, or personal diary-keeping or memoing or presentational writing. Though academic writing in its purest form has become polysemic in terms of style, it can still be distinguished from these other forms listed above. Furthermore, the writing style reflects a particular epistemic position taken up by the writer.

The academic realist text is a traditional form of academic writing in which the writer of the research report writes themselves out of the text. No reference is made to the autobiography of the writer, or to the context in which the data were collected. There is generally some methodological discussion that explains the way the data were collected and analysed. The assumption is made that the writer's own preferences, understandings of the world and ways of conceiving method can be put to one side during the data collection and analysis stages and do not contribute to the type of data collected. The text is linear, again usually presented as a series of stages: hypothesis formation, operationalizing of concepts, presentation of data, data analysis and conclusions/recommendations. All traces of the constructed nature of the text are erased thus giving the impression that the text stands in some unproblematic way for the reality it purports to describe.

A broken text, on the other hand, does not exhibit a linear form, but is broken up, discontinuous, comes to sudden endings, does not have a recognizable coherence to it. It is difficult to read as most readers are inducted into traditional forms of writing and therefore look for coherence where none is intended. Indeed, texts such as these are sometimes judged by conventional standards and usually found wanting. The rationale for such a textual form is that it seeks to convey the impression that the sequence of events it is attempting to describe does not take the form that the realist textual approach would suggest. If reality is unstructured, messy, serendipitous, then the text should convey this in the way it is written.

Van Maanan (1988) identifies another form of textuality, which can be distinguished from the academic realist form, where the authorial 'I' is privileged. The traditional academic text excludes the confessional or refers to it separately from the research report itself. Recently ethnographers have sought to provide confessional accounts of the research process and within these accounts justify the choices they made during the fieldwork period. This has by necessity included biographical data, though it is of course biographical data expressed in a traditional academic form. Some researchers would go beyond the merely attached confessional account and argue that the textually mediated reflexive stance needs to be more fundamental than this: 'Rather it is the effect of sociality and the inscription of the self in social practices, language and discourses which constitute the research process' (Usher 1996: 9).

The transparent text can be contrasted with opaque writing that seeks to conceal the reflexivity of the writer. Furthermore, it seeks to present itself as authoritative by using devices such as extensive but uncritical referencing, polemic, assertion, decontextualization both of data collection and analysis and a desire to conceal its epistemological and ontological frameworks with the intention of suggesting that these are unproblematic. The transparent text, on the other hand, shows its hand at every point and allows the reader to make a proper judgement about how the data were collected and how the conclusions the researcher came to were reached. It is transparent in that it does not (though this is rarely possible) seek to conceal its genesis as knowledge.

The dialogic text can be contrasted with the monologic text where the voice that is always privileged and given most emphasis is the voice of the researcher. The dialogic form refers to the depriveleging of the author's voice; equal standing being given to a multitude of voices. This may represent an aspiration rather than a reality since the authority of the author is always sustained in any text through the researcher's selection of voices, their central role in the data collection process and their choice of focus. However, the dialogic author attempts to minimize the extent of their role in the research and give expression to a large number of voices through quotation and minimal comment and analysis.

The distinction between 'readerly' and 'writerly' texts is one developed by Barthes (1975). He was concerned to suggest that a text may be deliberately constructed so that it allows the reader to write their own agenda into it during their reading of it. This is a 'writerly' text and can be contrasted with a 'readerly' text, which attempts to rule out or signal as incorrect alternative interpretations. No text is able absolutely to sustain itself as a prescriptive or 'readerly' text, not least in that the reader may simply ignore it altogether. However, the distinction here is intended to suggest that texts are constructed differently in terms of how much space is allowed to the reader to incorporate their own understandings of events and activities referred to in the text into the way they read those texts.

The polemical text seeks to persuade its audience that they should think in one way and not in another. It therefore does not engage in any form of internal debate. Evidence is presented selectively to support a particular case, and indeed if it is thought that persuasion is possible without reference to evidence and even that reference to evidence may weaken the polemical message, then the rhetorical message is deemed to be sufficient. Furthermore, no attempt is made to describe what is and then argue that this is where one should be, because accurate depictions of reality are not necessary if one is trying to persuade the reader to believe that this is what should be.

The report as a text is characterized differently. Here the purpose is technical, uni-dimensional, sparse, bereft of references to past work and to wider concerns. An argument is sustained by reiteration so that each point is made a number of times at different moments in the text. Above all, the report is recommendatory so that the purpose is to suggest a plan of action, which, if the report is accepted, will lead to changes in working practices, usually set out in terms of a number of definite steps. Bullet points are common, reflective writing is avoided and practical action is the main rationale for its production. Furthermore, audience receptivity is paramount so that it might include an executive summary for busy readers who cannot find the time to read the report in full; or the vocabulary and constructional devices are such that they are in tune with those used by the readership. For example, a report to parents from a school is written differently from one to the governors of that school. In other words, assumptions are made about the discourse community that the report is designed for.

The problem is fundamentally to do with writing and the forms of knowledge that this implies. Lam (2000: 490) suggests that there are epistemological distinctions between what he calls explicit and tacit knowledge. These differences take three forms. The first is that explicit knowledge is codified so that it can be 'abstracted, stored, traded and communicated – it can be objectified' (Taylor 2003: 26). Implicit knowledge, not in written form, is intuitive and unarticulated. It works by paying close attention to, and in close interaction with, the person to whom it is being transferred. The second distinction is that explicit knowledge 'can be acquired through formal study, and generated through reasoning' (Taylor 2003: 26). On the other hand, tacit knowledge is informally acquired through practical experience in the workplace. Finally, 'explicit knowledge can be accumulated and aggregated as objective information. . . . It is very difficult, if not impossible, to abstract it from its social and material context in authentic ways' (Taylor 2003: 26). Even if objectified knowledge is expressed in transparent, broken, confessional or 'readerly' forms, we are suggesting here that many of the workplaces from which professional doctorate students come do not work through formal, storable and objectified knowledge

Professional doctorates as we have seen are driven by a desire to change practice in some immediate sense. This would suggest that the production of a written text whether of a report, polemic, realist text or whatever, is only one part of this apparatus. Yet because the doctorate requires that work be accredited, evidence for meeting a standard to allow an award is usually inscribed. Second generation professional doctorates have sought to build a bridge to the workplace and to some extent validate workplace-based knowledge. This distinguishes them from first generation doctorates that sought to mimic the traditional PhD. The problem, not wholly resolved by the introduction of portfolios, is that evidence for changes in workplace practices still has to be inscribed in some form or other. Inscription by virtue of what it is changes the nature of the knowledge that is being constructed. It does this by building in an element of what we called in a previous chapter meta-reflection or reflection on reflection-in-action, and it does so by turning the knowledge-development activity into a retrospective affair. In turn, of course, this reflection on reflection-in-action may become a part of the action sequence, and can thus be construed as the practitioner's change to their practice. What is undeniable however, is that at some point, the knowledge process becomes reified, and is no longer a part of the ongoing construction of knowledge taking place within the workplace.

The other alternative is to assess changes to practice without evoking inscribed knowledge. This radical solution takes one beyond portfolios (and their inscribed practices), and indeed suggests that second generation doctorates will in time give way to a third generation doctorate where evidence for accreditation and validation is not gathered by thesis, dissertation or portfolio, but by observation or interview by the assessor of the changes to the workplace practices of the individual seeking accreditation for those changes. This alternative has a number of consequences for the university, and moves the university into uncharted territory. The logics of knowledge production here have certainly changed with a wholesale abandonment of disciplinary knowledge and a colonization by the workplace of academic knowledge. These changes would require the university to rethink in a fundamental sense their relationship with the workplace.

Conclusion

We have suggested above that the three principal innovative features of professional doctorates are the use of portfolio assessment, the designation of criteria for judging student performance that are specifically related to the various workplaces that students either already, or will, belong to, and radical forms of inscriptive or performative behaviours which are the end-points of doctoral study, and which form the products for accreditation. To these we can add features that have formed important themes in the preceding chapters: curriculum models that overtly specify learning outcomes (cf. UKCGE 2002); an understanding that effective learning environments need to both make explicit reference to workplace concerns and outcomes *and* be structured so that the type of knowledge produced as a result of professional doctorate study resonates with that produced in the workplace; and pedagogic forms which acknowledge previously acquired experiential knowledge and are co-constructed.

What are the implications of this for doctoral study? We close this book by suggesting four areas for reflection. The first of these is that workplace learners cannot by themselves develop the appropriate skills and capabilities for the knowledge economy. The second is that systematic reflection on one's own actions can only take place in scaffolded environments that are to some extent removed from the immediate sites of action. The third area is that the co-production of knowledge within a variety of discourse communities, difficult as it is to make connections between them, has the potential to enrich the workplace. Finally, it has to be acknowledged that many of the courses and programmes that we examined subscribed to a belief that students should be inducted into disciplinary knowledge structures, and that this would translate unproblematically into more effective workplace practices. This, as we have suggested in this book, is far from true. What universities need to do is to widen their epistemological perspectives, and embrace new forms of knowledge construction.

References

Allen, C., Smyth, E. and Wahlstrom, M. (2002) Responding to the field and to the academy: Ontario's Evolving PhD, *Higher Education Research and Development,* 21(2): 203–14.

Argyris, C. and Schon, D. (1978) *Theory in Practice: Increasing Professional Practice.* San Francisco, CA: Jossey-Bass.

Association of Business Schools (1998) *Guidelines for the Doctor of Business Administration Degree.* London: ABS.

Ball, S. (2001) Performativities and fabrications in the education economy: towards the performative society, in D. Gleeson and C. Husbands (eds) *The Performing School: Managing, Teaching and Learning in a Performance Culture.* London and New York: Routledge Falmer.

Bareham, J. and Bourner, T. (2000) The DBA: what is it for?, *Career Development International,* 5(7): 394–403.

Barnett, R. (1994) *The Limits of Competence: Knowledge, Higher Education and Society.* Buckingham: Open University Press.

Barnett, R. (1997) *Higher Education: A Critical Business.* Buckingham: Open University Press.

Barnett, R. (1999) *Realising the University in an Age of Supercomplexity.* Buckingham: Open University Press.

Barthes, R. (1975) *S/Z.* London: Jonathan Cape.

Baumgart, N. and Linfoot, K. (1998) The Professional doctorate in education: A new model, in T.W. Maxwell and P.J. Shanahan (eds) *Professional Doctorates: Innovations in Teaching and Research,* Proceedings of the Conference: Professional Doctorates: Innovations in Teaching and Research. Coffs Harbour, Faculty of Education, Health and Professional Studies, University of New England, Armidale.

Becher, T. (1999a) Universities and mid-career professionals: the policy potential, *Higher Education Quarterly,* 53(2): 156–72.

Becher, T. (1999b) Quality in the Professions, *Studies in Higher Education,* 24(2): 225–35.

Becher, T., Henkel, M. and Kogan, M. (1994) *Graduate Education in Britain.* London: Jessica Kingsley Publishers.

Bernstein, B. (1990) *The Structuring of Pedagogic Discourse.* London: Routledge.

Bernstein, B. (2000) *Pedagogy, Symbolic Control and Identity: Theory, Research, Critique*, revised edn. Lanham, Maryland: Rowman and Littlefield.

Bernstein, B. and Solomon, J. (1999) Pedagogy, identity and the construction of a theory of symbolic control: Basil Bernstein questioned by Joseph Solomon, *British Journal of Sociology of Education*, 20(2): 265–79.

Boud, D. and Garrick, J. (1999) *Understanding Learning at Work*. Routledge: London.

Boud, D. and Walker, D. (1990) Making the most of experience, *Studies in Continuing Education*, 12(2): 61–80.

Boud, D. and Walker, D. (1998) Promoting Reflection in Professional Courses: The Challenge of Context, *Studies in Higher Education*, 23(2): 191–206.

Bourner, T., Bowden, R. and Laing, S. (2000a) Professional doctorates: the development of researching professionals, in T. Bourner, T. Katz and D. Watson (eds) *New Directions in Professional Higher Education*. Buckingham: SRHE and Open University Press.

Bourner, T., Bowden, R. and Laing, S. (2000b) The adoption of professional doctorates in English universities: Why here? Why now? Paper presented at the 3rd Biennial International conference on professional doctorates, University of New England, September 2000.

Bourner, T., Bowden, R. and Laing, S. (2001a) Professional doctorates in England, *Studies in Higher Education*, 26(1): 65–83.

Bourner, T., Bowden, R. and Laing, S. (2001b) The adoption of professional doctorates in English universities: Why here? Why now?, in B. Green, T. Maxwell and P. Shanahan (eds) *Doctoral Education and Professional Practice: the Next Generation*. Australia: Kardoorair Press.

Bowden, R., Bourner, T. and Laing, S. (2002) Professional doctorates in England and Australia: not a world of difference, *Higher Education Review*, 35(1): 3–23.

Breen, R. and Lindsay, R. (1999) Academic Research and Student Motivation, *Studies in Higher Education*, 24(1): 75–93.

Brennan, M. (1998) Education doctorates: reconstructing professional partnerships around research?, in A. Lee and B. Green (eds) *Postgraduate Studies/Postgraduate Pedagogy*. Sydney: Centre for Language and Literacy and University Graduate School, University of Technology.

Brew, A. (2001) *The Nature of Research. Inquiry in Academic Contexts*. London: Routledge Falmer.

Brookfield, S.J. (1987) *Developing Critical Thinkers: Challenging Adults to Explore Alternative Ways of Thinking and Acting*. San Francisco: Jossey-Bass.

Brookfield, S. J. (1995) *Becoming a Critically Reflective Teacher*. San Francisco: Jossey-Bass.

Burgess, R.G. (1997) *Beyond the First Degree: Graduate Education, Lifelong Learning and Careers*. Buckingham: Open University Press.

Carter, B. (2000) *Realism and Racism*. London: Routledge.

Collinson, J. (1998) Professionally trained researchers? Expectations of competence in social science doctoral research training, *Higher Education Review*, 31(1): 59–67.

Cowan, R. (1997) Comparative perspectives on the British PhD, in N. Graves and V. Varma (eds) *Working for a Doctorate: A Guide for the Humanities and Social Sciences*. London: Routledge.

Dale, R. (1989) *The State and Education Policy*. Buckingham: Open University Press.

Dearing Report (1997) *The National Committee of Enquiry in Higher Education*. London: HMSO.

Deci, E.L. and Ryan, R.M. (1985) *Intrinsic Motivation and Self-determination in Human Behavior.* New York: Plenum.

Delamont, S., Atkinson, P. and Parry, O. (2000) *The Doctoral Experience: Success and Failure in Graduate School.* London: Falmer Press.

Delanty, G. (2001) *Challenging Knowledge: the University in the Knowledge Society.* Buckingham: Open University Press.

Donn, J., Routh, D. and Lunt, I. (2000) From Leipzig to Luxembourg (via Boulder and Vail): history of clinical psychology training in Europe and the United States, *Professional Psychology: Research and Practice,* 31(4): 423–8.

Economic and Social Research Council (2001) *Postgraduate Training Guidelines.* www.esrc.ac.uk/esrccontent/postgradfunding/postgraduatetrainingguidelines 2001.asp.

Elliott, B. and Hughes, C. (1998) Outcomes driven curriculum reform – reconstructing teacher work and professionalism. Paper presented at European Conference for Educational Research, Ljubljana, Slovenia, September.

Engineering and Physical Sciences Research Council (1997) *Review of the EPSRC Engineering Doctorate Pilot Scheme.* Swindon: Engineering and Physical Sciences Research Council.

Engineering and Physical Sciences Research Council Website www.epsrc.ac.uk (accessed January 2003).

Entwistle, N. and Ramsden, P. (1983) *Understanding Student Learning.* London: Croom Helm.

Eraut, M. (1994) *Developing Professional Knowledge and Competence.* Lewes: Falmer Press.

Evans, T. (1997) Flexible doctoral research: emerging issues in professional doctorate programs, *Studies in Continuing Education,* 19(2): 174–82.

Evers, C. and Lakomski, G. (1991) *Knowing Educational Administration: Contemporary Methodological Controversies in Educational Administration.* Oxford: Pergamon Press.

Finniston Report (1980) *Engineering our Future.* London: HMSO.

Foucault, M. (1977) *Discipline and Punish: The Birth of the Prison.* New York: Vintage.

Freire, P. (1972) *Pedagogy of the Oppressed.* Harmondsworth: Penguin.

General Medical Council (GMC) (2000) Revalidating doctors. Ensuring standards, securing the future. Consultation document for the General Medical Council. London: GMC.

General Teaching Council (GTC) (2002) The code of professional values and practice for teachers. Document produced by the General Teaching Council. London: GTC.

Gibbons, M., Limoges, C., Nowotny, H., Schwartzman, S., Scott, P. and Trow, M. (1994) *The New Production of Knowledge: The Dynamics of Science and Research in Contemporary Societies.* London: Sage.

Giddens, A. (1991) *Modernity and Self-Identity: Self and Society in the Late Modern Age.* Cambridge: Polity Press.

Green, B. and Lee, A. (1999) Educational research, disciplinarity and postgraduate pedagogy: on the subject of supervision, in A. Holbrook and S. Johnston (eds) *Supervision of PostGraduate Research in Education.* Coldstream, Victoria: Australian Association for Research in Education.

Gregory, M. (1997) Professional scholars and scholarly professionals, *The New Academic,* 19–22.

Guba, E. and Lincoln, Y. (1985) *Naturalistic Enquiry.* London: Sage.

Guba, E. and Lincoln, Y. (1989) *Fourth Generation Evaluation.* London: Sage.

Habermas, J. (1974) Rationalism divided in two, in A. Giddens (ed.) *Positivism and Sociology*. Aldershot: Gower Publishing Company Ltd.

Habermas, J. (1987) *Knowledge and Human Interests*. Cambridge: Polity Press.

Hall, V. (1996) When the going gets tough. Learning through a taught doctorate programme, in G. Claxton, T. Atkinson, M. Osborn and M. Wallace (eds) *Liberating the Learner*. London: Routledge.

Hammersley, M. (1992) *What's Wrong with Ethnography: Methodological Explorations*. London and New York: Routledge.

Hanlon, G. (1998) Professionalism as enterprise: service class politics and the redefinition of professionalism, *Sociology*, 32(1): 43–63.

Harris Report (1996) *Review of Postgraduate Education*. Bristol: HEFCE, CVCP.

Hesketh, A.J. and Knight, P.T. (1999) Postgraduates' choice of programme: helping universities to market and students to choose, *Studies in Higher Education*, 24(2): 151–63.

Holland, S. and Brown, C. (2000) Learning, earning and working: insights from service professionals seeking research training. Paper presented at the 3rd Biennial International Conference on Professional Doctorates, University of New England, September 2000.

Humphrey, R. and McCarthy, P. (1999) Recognising difference: providing for postgraduate students, *Studies in Higher Education*, 24(3): 371–86.

Jarvis, P. (2000) The changing university: meeting a need and needing to change, *Higher Education Quarterly*, 54(1): 43–67.

Joint Funding Council (2003) *The Development of Research and other Skills*. London: JFC.

Kendall, G. (2002) The crisis in doctoral education: a sociological diagnosis, *Higher Education Research and Development*, 21(2): 131–41.

Lam, A. (2000) Tacit knowledge, organisational learning and social institutions: an integrated framework, *Organisational Studies*, 21: 487–513.

Landow, G. (1992) *The Convergence of Contemporary Critical Theory and Technology*. Baltimore and London: The Johns Hopkins University Press.

Latour, B. (1987) *Science in Action: How to Follow Engineers in Society*. Buckingham: Open University Press.

Lave, J. and Wenger, E. (1991) *Situated Learning: Legitimate Peripheral Participation*. Cambridge: Cambridge University Press.

Lee, A. (1999) Research and knowledge in the professional doctorate. Paper presented at Symposium: *Professional Doctorates in New Times for the Australian University*, AARE, Brisbane, December 1997.

Lee, A., Green, B. and Brennan, M. (2000) Organisational knowledge, professional practice and the professional doctorate at work, in J. Garrick and C. Rhodes (eds) *Research and Knowledge at Work: Perspectives, Case-studies and Innovative Strategies*. London: Routledge.

Lunt, I. (2002) Professional doctorates in education. 'State of the art' paper commissioned by ESCalate and available on ESCalate website www.escalate.ac.uk

Lyotard, J.F. (1984) *The Postmodern Condition: A Report on Knowledge*. Manchester: Manchester University Press.

Marshall, J. (1990) Foucault and Educational Research, in S. Ball (ed.) *Foucault and Education: Disciplines and Knowledge*. London: Routledge.

Maslow, A. (1954) *Motivation and Personality*. New York: Harper & Row.

Maxwell, T.W. (2003a) Writing in/up a professional doctorate portfolio/dissertation, in E. McWilliam (ed.) *Research Training for the Knowledge Economy*. Brisbane, Australia: University of Brisbane.

Maxwell, T.W. (2003b) From first to second generation professional doctorate, *Studies in Higher Education* 28(3): 279–91.

Maxwell, T.W. and Shanahan, P.J. (1997) Towards a reconceptualisation of the doctorate: issues arising from comparative data relating to the EdD in Australia, *Studies in Higher Education* 22(2): 133–50.

Maxwell, T.W. and Shanahan, P.J. (2000) Current issues in professional doctoral education in Australia and New Zealand. Paper presented at the 3rd Biennial International Conference on Professional Doctorates, University of New England, September 2000.

McNair, S. (1997) Is there a crisis? Does it matter?, in R. Barnett and A. Griffin (eds) *The End of Knowledge in Higher Education*. London: Cassell.

McWilliam, E., Singh, P. and Taylor, P. (2002), Doctoral education, danger and risk management, *Higher Education Research & Development*, 21(2): 120–9.

Mead, G.H. (1964) *Social Psychology*. London and Chicago: Phoenix Books and University of Chicago Press.

Metcalfe, J., Thompson, Q. and Green, H. (2002), *Improving Standards in Postgraduate Research Degree Programmes: A Report to the Higher Education Funding Councils of England, Scotland and Wales*. Bristol: HEFCE.

Naccarato, R. (1988) *Assessing Learning Motivation: A Consumers' Guide*. Portland, Oregon: North West Regional Educational Laboratory.

Neave, G. (1988) On the cultivation of quality, efficiency and enterprise: an overview of recent trends in higher education in Western Europe, *European Journal of Education*, 23(1/2): 7–23.

Noble, K.A. (1994) *Changing Doctoral Degrees. An International Perspective*. Buckingham: SRHE and Open University Press.

Office of Science and Technology (1993) *White Paper on Research Policy*. London: OST.

Pearson, M. (1999) The changing environment for doctoral education in Australia: implications for quality management, improvement and innovation, *Higher Education Research and Development*, 18(3): 269–87.

Pintrich, P.R. and Schunk, D.H. (1996) *Motivation in Education. Theory, Research & Applications*. Englewood Cliffs, NJ: Prentice-Hall.

Poole, M. and Spear, R.H. (1997) Policy issues in postgraduate education: an Australian perspective, in R.G. Burgess (ed.) *Beyond the First Degree: Graduate Education, Lifelong Learning and Careers*. Buckingham: SRHE and Open University Press.

Quality Assurance Agency (1999) *Code of Practice for the Assurance of Academic Quality and Standards in Higher Education: Postgraduate Research Programmes*. London: QAA.

Quality Assurance Agency (2001) *The National Qualifications Framework for Higher Education Qualifications in England, Wales and Northern Ireland*. London: QAA.

Reich, R.B. (1993) *The Work of Nations: a Blueprint for the Future*. London: Simon & Schuster.

Research Councils and Arts and Humanities Research Board (2002) *Skills Training Requirements for Research Students*. London: RC and AHRB.

Ruggeri-Stevens, G., Bareham, J. and Bourner, T. (2001) The DBA in British universities: assessment and standards, *Quality Assurance in Education*, 9(2): 61–71.

Schon, D. (1983) *The Reflective Practitioner*. London: Temple Smith.

Schon, D. (1987) *Educating the Reflective Practitioner*. San Francisco: Jossey-Bass.

Scott, D. and Lunt, I. (2000) Curriculum and assessment issues with professional doctorates, in D. Scott (ed.) *Curriculum and Assessment*. Westport: Greenwood Publishing Group Inc.

Scott, D., Brown, A., Lunt, I. and Thorne, L. (2003) Integrating academic and professional knowledge: constructing the practitioner-researcher, in E. McWilliam (ed.) *Research Training for the Knowledge Economy*. Brisbane, Australia: University of Brisbane.

Scott, P. (2000) The crisis of knowledge and the massification of higher education, in R. Barnett and A. Griffin (eds) *The End of Knowledge in Higher Education*. London: Cassell.

Seddon, T. (2000) What is doctoral in doctoral education? Paper presented at the 3rd International Professional Doctorates Conference, Doctoral Education and Professional Practice: the Next Generation? Armidale, 10–12 September.

Senge, P. (1990) *The Fifth Discipline*. New York: Doubleday.

Shulman, L. (1987) *Paradigms and Programs: Research in Teaching and Learning, Volume 1*. New York: Macmillan.

Smith, P.R. (2002) A meeting of cultures: part-time students in an EdD program, *International Journal of Leadership in Education*, 3(4): 359–80.

Taylor, J. (2002) Changes in teaching and learning in the period to 2005: the case of postgraduate education in the UK, *Journal of Higher Education Policy and Management*, 24(1): 53–73.

Taylor, P. (2003) Research training for industry-based workers, in E. McWilliam (ed.) *Research Training for the Knowledge Economy*, Brisbane, Australia: University of Brisbane.

Thorne, L.E. (1999) Perspectives on the purposes, processes and products of doctorates: towards a rich picture of doctorates. Unpublished PhD thesis, Middlesex University.

Thorne, L.E. (2001) Doctoral level learning: customisation for communities of practice, in B. Green, T.W. Maxwell and P. Shanahan (eds) *Doctoral Education and Professional Practice: the Next Generation*. Armidale: Kardoorair Press.

Tooley, J. and Darby, D. (1998) *Educational Research: A Critique, a Survey of Published Educational Research*. London: Office for Standards in Education.

Trigwell, K., Shannon, T. and Maurizi, R. (1997) Research-course doctoral programs in Australian universities. Canberra: Evaluations and Investigations program, Higher Education Division, Department of Employment, Education, Training and Youth Affairs.

UK Council for Graduate Education (1998) *The Status of Published Work in Submissions for Doctoral Degrees in European Universities*. Warwick: UKCGE.

UK Council for Graduate Education (2002) *Report on Professional Doctorates*. Dudley: UKCGE.

Usher, R. (1996) A critique of the neglected assumptions of educational research, in D. Scott and R. Usher (eds) *Understanding Educational Research*. London: Routledge.

Usher, R. (1997) Telling a story about research and research as story-telling: postmodern approaches to social research, in G. McKenzie, J. Powell and R. Usher (eds) *Understanding Social Research: Perspectives on Methodology and Practice*. London: Falmer Press.

Usher, R. (2002) A Diversity of doctorates: fitness for the knowledge economy, *Higher Education Research and Development*, 21(2): 143–53.

Usher, R., Bryant, I. and Johnston, R. (1997) *Adult Education and the Post-modern Challenge: Learning Beyond the Limits*. London: Routledge.

Van Maanen, M. (1988) *Tales of the Field: On Writing Ethnography*. Chicago: Chicago University Press.

Walsh, P. (1993) *Education and Meaning: Philosophy in Practice.* London: Cassell.

Watson, D. (2000) Lifelong learning and professional higher education, in T. Bourner, T. Katz and D. Watson (eds) *New Directions in Professional Education.* Buckingham: SRHE and Open University Press.

Wenger, E. (1998) *Communities of Practice: Learning, Meaning and Identity.* Cambridge: Cambridge University Press.

Whitty, G. (2001) Teacher professionalism in new times, in D. Gleeson and C. Husbands (eds) *The Performing School: Managing, Teaching and Learning in a Performance Culture.* London and New York: Routledge Falmer.

Winfield Enquiry (1987) *The Social Science PhD: the ESRC Enquiry on Submission Rates.* London: Economic and Social Research Council.

Winter, R., Griffiths, M. and Green, K. (2000) *The academic Qualities of Practice: What are the Criteria for a Practice-based PhD?* London: Advisory Group for Continuing Education and Life-Long Learning, HMSO.

Wlodkowski, R.J. (1985) *Enhancing Adult Motivation to Learn.* San Francisco, CA: Jossey-Bass.

Yeatman, A. (1990) *Bureaucrats, Technocrats, Femocrats: Essays on the Contemporary Australian State.* Sydney: Allen and Unwin.

Yeatman, A. (1996) Developing critical literacy in different kinds of research. Proceedings of the NSW HIV/AIDS Health Promotion Conference, Sydney, November 1995.

Index

The Society for Research into Higher Education

The Society for Research into Higher Education (SRHE), an international body, exists to stimulate and coordinate research into all aspects of higher education. It aims to improve the quality of higher education through the encouragement of debate and publication on issues of policy, on the organization and management of higher education institutions, and on the curriculum, teaching and learning methods.

The Society is entirely independent and receives no subsidies, although individual events often receive sponsorship from business or industry. The Society is financed through corporate and individual subscriptions and has members from many parts of the world. It is an NGO of UNESCO.

Under the imprint *SRHE & Open University Press*, the Society is a specialist publisher of research, having over 80 titles in print. In addition to *SRHE News*, the Society's newsletter, the Society publishes three journals: *Studies in Higher Education* (three issues a year), *Higher Education Quarterly* and *Research into Higher Education Abstracts* (three issues a year).

The Society runs frequent conferences, consultations, seminars and other events. The annual conference in December is organized at and with a higher education institution. There are a growing number of networks which focus on particular areas of interest, including:

Access	FE/HE
Assessment	Graduate Employment
Consultants	New Technology for Learning
Curriculum Development	Postgraduate Issues
Eastern European	Quantitative Studies
Educational Development Research	Student Development

Benefits to members

Individual

- The opportunity to participate in the Society's networks
- Reduced rates for the annual conferences
- Free copies of *Research into Higher Education Abstracts*
- Reduced rates for *Studies in Higher Education*

- Reduced rates for *Higher Education Quarterly*
- Free online access to *Register of Members' Research Interests* – includes valuable reference material on research being pursued by the Society's members
- Free copy of occasional in-house publications, e.g. *The Thirtieth Anniversary Seminars Presented by the Vice-Presidents*
- Free copies of *SRHE News* and *International News* which inform members of the Society's activities and provides a calendar of events, with additional material provided in regular mailings
- A 35 per cent discount on all SRHE/Open University Press books
- The opportunity for you to apply for the annual research grants
- Inclusion of your research in the *Register of Members' Research Interests*

Corporate

- Reduced rates for the annual conference
- The opportunity for members of the Institution to attend SRHE's network events at reduced rates
- Free copies of *Research into Higher Education Abstracts*
- Free copies of *Studies in Higher Education*
- Free online access to *Register of Members' Research Interests* – includes valuable reference material on research being pursued by the Society's members
- Free copy of occasional in-house publications
- Free copies of *SRHE News* and *International News*
- A 35 per cent discount on all SRHE/Open University Press books
- The opportunity for members of the Institution to submit applications for the Society's research grants
- The opportunity to work with the Society and co-host conferences
- The opportunity to include in the *Register of Members' Research Interests* your Institution's research into aspects of higher education

Membership details: SRHE, 76 Portland Place, London W1B 1NT, UK Tel: 020 7637 2766. Fax: 020 7637 2781. email: srheoffice@srhe.ac.uk
world wide web: http://www.srhe.ac.uk./srhe/
Catalogue: SRHE & Open University Press, McGraw-Hill Education, McGraw-Hill House, Shoppenhangers Road, Maidenhead, Berkshire SL6 2QL. Tel: 01628 502500. Fax: 01628 770224. email: enquiries@openup.co.uk
web: www.openup.co.uk

THE DOCTORAL EXAMINATION PROCESS
A Handbook for Students, Examiners and Supervisors

Penny Tinkler and Caroline Jackson

- What is the viva and how can students prepare for it?
- What should supervisors consider when selecting PhD examiners?
- How should examiners assess a doctoral thesis and conduct the viva?

The doctoral examination process has been shrouded in mystery and has been a frequent source of anxiety and concern for students, supervisors and examiners alike. But now help is at hand. This book sheds new light on the process, providing constructive ways of understanding the doctoral examination, preparing for it and undertaking it.

This book stands alone in the field due to the extensive research undertaken by the authors. During a four year project, interviews were conducted with candidates and academics from a wide range of disciplines through the United Kingdom. Outcomes and ideas from the research have been united to provide the most comprehensive information available.

Real life accounts and case studies are combined with useful advice, tasks and checklists to create an illuminating handbook. This user-friendly book is a vital resource for anyone involved in the doctoral process. No doctoral candidate, examiner or supervisor should be without it.

Contents

192pp   0 335 21305 7 (Paperback)   0 335 21306 5 (Hardback)

NEW DIRECTIONS IN PROFESSIONAL HIGHER EDUCATION

Tom Bourner, Tim Katz and David Watson (eds)

This book exemplifies the growing involvement of universities in professional education at its highest level. It also demonstrates the increasing importance of education for the professions in the work of universities.

It contains a wealth of practical examples and ideas about how universities can respond to the changing needs of students' initial professional training, continuing professional development and lifelong learning.

At the heart of the book is a series of analytical case studies of developing practices that respond to the challenges to higher education at the start of the new millennium. These chapters address important themes in developing professional HE: partnership, independent learning, reflective practice, new technologies, intranets, world wide web, distance learning, the international dimension, work readiness, assessment and standards. Many of the case studies test out ideas in action.

The result is a valuable handbook for practitioners of professional education in HE and an important resource for staff and educational developers and higher education managers.

Contents

Foreword – Preface and Acknowledgements – Part One: Setting the Scene – Life long learning and professional higher education – Issues of professionalism in higher education – University education for developing professional practice – Part Two: Case Studies – Partnership in higher education – Independent learning and reflective practice – Using the new learning technologies – Using the Internet and the world wide web – Distance learning and the international dimension – Preparation for professional practice – Assessment and Standards – Part Three: New Directions – A framework for personal and professional development – Professional doctorates: the development of researching professionals – Practitioner centred research – References – Index.

272pp   0 335 20614 X (Paperback)   0 335 20615 8 (Hardback)

CHALLENGING KNOWLEDGE
Gerard Delanty

For far too long, we have waited for a book that recorded the ideas of the modern university. Now, in Gerard Delanty's new book, we have it. Delanty has faithfully set out the views of the key thinkers and, in the process, has emerged with an idea of the university that is his. We are in his debt.

Professor Ronald Barnett, University of London

Gerard Delanty is one of the most productive and thought-provoking social theorists currently writing in the UK. He brings to his work a sophisticated and impressively cosmopolitan vision. Here he turns his attention to higher education, bringing incisive analysis and a surprising optimism as regards the future of the university. This is a book which will stimulate all thinking people – especially those trying to come to terms with mass higher education and its tribulations.

Professor Frank Webster, University of Birmingham

For too long social theory, the sociology of knowledge and studies in higher education have mutually ignored each other. Gerard Delanty, founding editor of the *European Journal of Social Theory*, was just the right person to bring them into dialogue. Indeed 'dialogue' and 'communication' are his watchwords for revamping the institutional mission of the university.

Professor Steve Fuller, University of Warwick

Drawing from current debates in social theory about the changing nature of knowledge, this book offers the most comprehensive sociological theory of the university that has yet appeared. Delanty views the university as a key institution of modernity and as the site where knowledge, culture and society interconnect. He assesses the question of the crisis of the university with respect to issues such as globalization, the information age, the nation state, academic capitalism, cultural politics and changing relationships between research and teaching. Arguing against the notion of the demise of the university, his argument is that in the knowledge society of today a new identity for the university is emerging based on communication and new conceptions of citizenship. It will be essential reading for those interested in changing relationships between modernity, knowledge, higher education and the future of the university.

Contents

192pp   0 335 20578 X (Paperback)   0 335 20579 8 (Hardback)